THE SOCIETY OF NATIONS

ITS PAST, PRESENT, AND POSSIBLE FUTURE

BY

T. J. LAWRENCE, LL.D., J.P.

MEMBER OF THE INSTITUTE OF INTERNATIONAL LAW;
HONORARY FELLOW OF DOWNING COLLEGE, CAMBRIDGE;
READER IN INTERNATIONAL LAW IN THE UNIVERSITY OF BRISTOL;
RECTOR OF UPTON LOVEL, WILTS;
LATE LECTURER ON INTERNATIONAL LAW AT THE ROYAL NAVAL WAR COLLEGE;
SOMETIME PROFESSOR OF INTERNATIONAL LAW IN THE UNIVERSITY OF CHICAGO;
AUTHOR OF "PRINCIPLES OF INTERNATIONAL LAW,"
"WAR AND NEUTRALITY IN THE FAR EAST," ETC.

FIRST EDITION

THE LAWBOOK EXCHANGE, LTD.
Clark, New Jersey
2005

ISBN 1-58477-562-9

Printed in the United States of America on acid-free paper

The Lawbook Exchange, Ltd.
33 Terminal Avenue
Clark, New Jersey 07066-1321

Please see our website for a selection of our other publications and fine facsimile reprints of classic works of legal history:
www.lawbookexchange.com

Library of Congress Cataloging-in-Publication Data

Lawrence, T. J. (Thomas Joseph), 1849-1919.
The society of nations : its past, present, and possible future / by T.J. Lawrence.-- 1st ed.
p. cm.
Originally published: 1st ed. New York : Oxford University Press, American Branch, 1919.
Includes bibliographical references and index.
ISBN 1-58477-562-9 (cloth : alk. paper)
1. League of Nations. 2. International relations. 3. International organization. 4. International law. I. Title.

JZ4871.L39 2005
341.22--dc22 2004057780

THE SOCIETY OF NATIONS

ITS PAST, PRESENT, AND POSSIBLE FUTURE

BY

T. J. LAWRENCE, LL.D., J.P.

MEMBER OF THE INSTITUTE OF INTERNATIONAL LAW;
HONORARY FELLOW OF DOWNING COLLEGE, CAMBRIDGE;
READER IN INTERNATIONAL LAW IN THE UNIVERSITY OF BRISTOL;
RECTOR OF UPTON LOVEL, WILTS;
LATE LECTURER ON INTERNATIONAL LAW AT THE ROYAL NAVAL WAR COLLEGE;
SOMETIME PROFESSOR OF INTERNATIONAL LAW IN THE UNIVERSITY OF CHICAGO;
AUTHOR OF "PRINCIPLES OF INTERNATIONAL LAW,"
"WAR AND NEUTRALITY IN THE FAR EAST," ETC.

FIRST EDITION

NEW YORK
OXFORD UNIVERSITY PRESS
AMERICAN BRANCH: 35 WEST 32ND STREET
LONDON, TORONTO, MELBOURNE, AND BOMBAY
1919

TO

J. W. THOMSON WALKER, Esq.,
M.B., C.M. (Edin.), F.R.C.S. (Eng.)

IN THANKFUL REMEMBRANCE OF A GREAT BENEFIT
MOST GENEROUSLY CONFERRED
ON THE AUTHOR

PREFACE

As Reader of International Law in the University of Bristol I have the privilege of lecturing there from time to time on such subjects connected with the *Jus Gentium* as seem to need elucidation at the moment. Happily I am not condemned to adapt myself to the requirements of an Examination Schedule, but am free to dwell on what fills my own mind and interests my audience, without regard to its value as a winner of marks. In the enjoyment of this freedom I gave six lectures in the Autumn of 1917 on *The Society of Nations*. Their substance is reproduced in the present volume, and to a large extent their wording also. But I have added a considerable amount of new matter, and have felt myself at liberty to introduce references to events that have taken place since the course was concluded. In fact, the growth of opinion on the great issues at stake in the present world-conflict has been so rapid, that in order to keep pace with it I have had to rewrite entirely and lengthen greatly the fifth and sixth lectures, which deal with the much-discussed proposal to create a League of Nations. What I said in the Council Chamber of the University of Bristol is in the book, but not exactly as I said it. The lectures have undergone some excision and much amplification.

The relations subsisting between independent states, and the rules of conduct they should observe in their mutual intercourse, have been till lately deemed by the ordinary intelligent citizen matters far beyond his ken.

He supposed they were very difficult and obscure, and simply declined to trouble himself about them. Now, under stress of the miseries caused by the present war, quite a new attitude is taken up. There is a tendency to look seriously into these matters in order to discover remedies for the evils that are threatening civilisation itself because of the unsatisfactory nature of inter-state relations. Nothing but good can come of this awakening, if it is accompanied by some real knowledge of the conditions under which the problems to be solved have grown up, and the circumstances that must be reckoned with in any serious attempt at their solution.

In the lectures which follow I have tried to supply some outlines of this knowledge. They are an attempt to meet the needs of intelligent people who neither possess nor wish to possess the technical skill of the historian or the jurist, but nevertheless desire to learn enough of what has taken place between states during the course of recorded history to enable them to form reasonable convictions with regard to the possibilities of improvement, and the lines along which mankind may advance towards it. I have endeavoured to show that there is a real Society of Nations, that it grew up by a gradual process of evolution which can be followed historically, and that it was on the point of developing certain much needed judicial and legislative organs when the present war brought about a crisis in its life, and placed before it the choice of making a long step forward in the path of progress or heading back towards barbarism and misery. Finally, I have tried to indicate the true line of advance and the best means of facilitating the march along it. My profound conviction is that the great fundamental factor in the whole complicated problem is moral and spiritual. If the nations are content to go on with their enmities and jealousies, their belief that the foremost places in the world, and the largest share of its material and intellectual good, are the prize of those who can most cleverly outwit and most efficiently outfight their neighbours, then there is nothing left for mankind but a swift descent into the abyss. But if they will substitute brotherhood for enmity, and mutual service for jealousy, and install justice instead of force as the ultimate arbiter in their disputes, they may rid the human race of some of its most crying evils, and inaugurate a better epoch of peace and prosperity.

In the early stages of the war I endeavoured to set forth some of these views in the pages of *Goodwill,* the organ of the British Council of the World Alliance for promoting international friendship through the Churches; and I am indebted to the Editor, the Rev. T. H. Rushbrooke, M.A., for permission to use a few small portions of my articles in the composition of the present lectures. To my lifelong friend Dr. Courtney S. Kenny, till lately Downing Professor of English Law in the University of Cambridge, and to my old pupil and valued fellow-labourer, Dr. A. Pearce Higgins, the learned editor of the last edition of Hall's *International Law,* I tender my grateful thanks for information which I should with difficulty, if at all, have obtained without their aid.

T. J. LAWRENCE.

Upton Lovel Rectory,
Wiltshire, England.
October 1st, 1918.

ANALYTICAL OUTLINE OF THE LECTURES.

LECTURE I.

The Origin of International Society.

Distinctions between the nation and the state. International Society involves

1. A considerable number of states.
2. The existence in each of ideas and standards sufficiently alike to enable them to understand each other and arrange for common action.
3. Territorial Sovereignty.

These essentials did not co-exist in the world till the period of the Renaissance and the Reformation, though long before we can discern a few customary rules applicable to war between states and to what we now call diplomacy.

The code which attempts to regulate interstate relations derived its rules originally from

Roman Law
Canon Law
Customs
Christian Morality

It came into being through the work of great writers, among whom may be specially mentioned

1. Francis Suarez (1548-1617), a Jesuit theologian.
2. Albericus Gentilis (1552-1608), a Protestant civilian.
3. Hugo Grotius (1583-1645), a Dutch Scholar, Jurist, Theologian, Publicist and Poet.

Grotius has been called the Father of International Law. A brief statement of what he accomplished.

LECTURE II.

The Growth of International Society.

International Society has grown enormously since the time of Grotius, and its leading members have been distinguished from the rest under the name of Great Powers. Its development has led to a corresponding development of International Law. The chief means whereby progress was made were

1. The theories of the Philosophical Jurists—Pufendorf, Wolff, Bynkershoek, Vattel, and others. Nature and her Law.
2. The succession of great Publicists. Their authority.
3. The development of Maritime International Law by Courts.
4. The addition of express consent to tacit consent. Law-Making Treaties.

LECTURE III.

International Society as it stood in July, 1914.

During the last three centuries International Law increased greatly in bulk, and a very rudimentary and imperfect International Legislature came into existence in the shape of the Hague Conferences of 1899 and 1907. When on July 31, 1914, Germany sent her ultimatum to Russia, the civilised world possessed

1. The beginnings of an Arbitral Jurisprudence.
2. A rapidly increasing "Statute Book of the Law of Nations."

Moreover, attempts had been made, with more or less success, to

1. Codify the Law of War on Land by means of the Hague *Règlement.*
2. Settle parts of the Law of War at Sea by some of the Hague Conventions of 1907, the Declaration of London of 1909, and the Oxford *Manuel* of 1913.
3. Create an International Prize Court and an International Judicial Arbitration Court.

But the hopeful prospect was vitiated by

1. The absence of any general obligation to enforce accepted rules.
2. The rapid and enormous advance in the application of science to warfare, and the organisation of nations for war.
3. The German doctrine of *Kriegsraison.*

LECTURE IV.

The Partial Overthrow of International Law.

The weak points referred to in the previous lectures have been accentuated during the present war by

1. The blow to good faith and the Obligation of Treaties struck by the German attack on Belgium.
2. The blow to Humanity and the Obligation of Law in general struck by German "frightfulness."
3. The blow to Neutral Rights struck by the widespread application of the doctrine of Reprisals.

The fabric of International Law has been badly shattered in some parts, but left standing in others. The parts reduced to ruin are

1. The Law of War.
2. The Law of Neutrality.

The parts but little touched are

1. The Law of Jurisdiction.
2. The Law of Diplomacy.

The downfall of a large portion of a building may weaken the rest. But on the other hand the desire of civilised humanity, not to destroy International Law, but to improve and strengthen it, is shewn by the fact that nearly the whole world has armed, or is arming, in its defence.

LECTURE V.

The Conditions of Reconstruction.

The work of building up the shattered edifice of International Law concerns the whole of civilised humanity. It is rendered imperative not only by German "frightfulness," but also by three recent developments,

1. The practical obliteration of the difference between combatants and non-combatants.
2. The creation of War Zones on the high seas.
3. The introduction of aerial warfare.

There are also three other points to be considered, the general effect of which is to make a new international order urgent as well as imperative.

1. The present opportunity is most favourable. If it is allowed to slip mankind may never have another.
2. The general and express consent of states is the only possible agent of immediate reform.
3. The world must be organized for peace rather than for war, and the duty of helping to enforce International Law must be laid on all states.

The following suggestions are put forth as to procedure:

1. The great Conference which meets to make peace should decide on the principal features of the new World-Order, and then appoint an International Committee to work out the details and another to revise and codify International Law.
2. Their Reports should be submitted to a great International Congress composed of representatives of all civilised states.
3. Without waiting for the completion of this process in all its details an international authority or authorities should be set up immediately to decide disputes which cannot be settled by diplomatic means.

LECTURE VI.

The Rebuilding of International Society.

A great change of heart among the peoples is necessary before a righteous international order can be set up. Brotherhood must drive away jealousy, and mutual service must take the place of mutual ill-will. The best available means for maintaining peaceful relations and diminishing the frequency and the horrors of war is the establishment of a League of Nations in which all or most civilised states shall bind themselves together for the purpose of settling disputes by justice instead of force. To this two fundamental objections are made.

1. It will be fatal to state sovereignty. A careful discussion shews this has no solid foundation.
2. It will be found impracticable. This can be met by shewing that the elements of the new order exist already and require only development and combination.

But undoubtedly these are serious difficulties, and they will tax to the full the best mental and moral elements in human nature. The problem is at bottom spiritual. The two organisations which can do the most to solve it are the Church and the Labour Movement.

THE SOCIETY OF NATIONS

LECTURE I.

THE ORIGIN OF INTERNATIONAL SOCIETY.

Before I begin to deal with the subject-matter of these lectures it seems desirable to make clear that the responsibility for the statements and arguments they contain is mine alone. The University of Bristol has arranged for their delivery; but its corporate action goes no further. It must not be held bound by my assertions, still less by the conclusions I draw from them. Most of my facts are the common property of all students who have investigated the history of international relations. My views are, I believe, shared by a rapidly increasing number of thoughtful people; but the responsibility for their utterance on the present occasion rests on no shoulders but my own.

This afternoon I am to speak about the origin of the Society of Nations. The average human being takes such a Society for granted, pretty much as he takes for granted families, governments, laws and tribunals. Yet all these owe their existence in their present shape to a long process of gradual development; and this is true of the Society of Nations also. There was a time when it was not. And when it came into existence it did not take at first, or indeed for generations afterwards, the form we knew before the World-War complicated or upset our previous notions. Moreover in its case we have to face the additional complication that the name does not properly fit the thing it is used to denote. If we were strictly accurate we should speak of the Society of States, not the Society of Nations. The usual phrase has obtained such a hold that we cannot avoid using it; but a little consideration will shew that it is unscientific and incorrect.

Nations are aggregations of individuals bound together by ties of common blood, common language, common history, common institutions, common religion, and a common way of looking at life and society. One or more of these characteristics may be wanting, and yet the rest may be sufficiently strong to create a bond between those who possess them much closer than any that unites them with the rest of the world. The Swiss, for instance, have neither a common religious faith nor a common tongue. But the ties of political freedom, historical association and geographical contiguity are so strong that no one in or out of Switzerland doubts for a moment the existence of a Swiss nation. Yet a nation is not necessarily a political unit, nor need it, or any part of it, be ruled by its own people. The Poles are split up into three great divisions no one of which is under distinctly Polish government. There is a German Poland, a Russian Poland, and an Austrian

Poland, but there is nowhere a Polish Poland.[1] On the other hand the Italian people live, as regards by far the greatest number of them, under rulers of their own race and their own choosing; but there is still on the borders of Italy an *Italia Irridenta* under Austrian domination.[1] Sometimes, as in the instances we have just been considering, the great bulk of a nation dwell together on a given portion of the earth's surface, which is peopled mainly, if not exclusively, by them. But there are cases where two or more nations are inextricably mingled in the same territory. Of certain districts in the Balkan Peninsula it is impossible to say that they are Greek or Bulgarian or Slav. They are all three in varying proportions, and the question which race is in a majority in any given place is often fiercely disputed, and proves in practice almost impossible of solution, owing to the feuds and subterfuges of the inhabitants. In such circumstances it is difficult, if not impossible, to make the nations concerned into separate self-governing units. And though the principle of nationality asserts that, wherever possible, this should be done, even at the cost of much regrouping of peoples and rearrangement of political boundaries, yet those who have adopted it as a working rule would be the last to assert that it can be applied universally.

We have seen that a nation is a group based on unity of sentiment or unity of blood, or both. On the other hand a state is a group based on unity of government.

[1] In the interval between the writing and the printing of these sentences they have happily lost their original accuracy.

When the two groups coincide, there is more prospect of stability and happiness than under any other political conditions. But when it is a question of regulating the relations between the various bodies into which mankind are divided for purposes of internal order and external security, it is the state rather than the nation that must be considered. Imagine an attempt to send an Ambassador to the Jews. Where is he to go? To whom is he to be accredited? Who has power to bind the Jewish nation to any agreement he may endeavour to negotiate? The same questions may be put, with the same impossibility of obtaining an answer, in respect of any nation which is not a state also, that is to say a group of people settled on a given portion of the earth's surface, and organised for purposes of government under rulers who have authority to speak for the whole body-politic in its dealings with other groups of the same nature. The intercourse of these groups is interstate intercourse. The society they form is a Society of States, not a Society of Nations. The rules they observe in their mutual relations are Interstate Law, not International Law.

It is necessary to remember this always, though we cannot now alter the nomenclature that has been in use for generations. But we ought to use it with the mental reservation that it signifies something which may or may not be identical with what it says. We are dealing to-day, and throughout this course, with states. And though probably all of us believe that in an ideal world states would invariably coincide with nations, we know that at present instances to the contrary abound. There are many states that are not nations and many nations that are not states. And though one result of the present World-War will almost certainly be an increase in the number of Nation States, we cannot suppose that it will blot out from the map all the states that are bundles of nationalities, or unite the severed parts of all nations that are now divided among two or more states. A completely satisfactory adjustment of the relations between state and nation cannot take place till many difficult problems connected with Federal Government on the one hand, and the control and development of backward races on the other, have been solved. I have no intention of discussing them now. But I do want to make it quite plain that at present we have no right to think of nations as the units of what we cannot escape from calling international society. In discussing this society, and the laws which do regulate, or ought to regulate, its affairs, we are dealing with states. We must use the old terms; but if we are to think clearly we must use them with the reservations I have insisted on.

Having dealt with this preliminary point, we can now go on to consider the conditions that must be satisfied before any real Society of Nations can exist and flourish. First, it is clear that a Society implies members. If all the world were one great state, there could not be a Society of States. This was exactly what occurred throughout the long centuries during which the dominion of the Roman Cæsars extended over all, or very nearly all, the civilised peoples of the earth. The existence of a common superior prevented the growth of separate and independent political units. States as we understand them could not, and did not, exist. Now the area of civilisation is far wider than it was in the palmiest days of ancient Rome. But it is broken up into a number of commonwealths, great and small, each of which acknowledges no earthly superior. These are constantly brought into relationship with each other, and form what is sometimes called the Family of Nations and sometimes the Society of Nations. Unless they existed together, and in constant contact with one another, International Law and all that it implies would be impossible. There can be no body of rules to regulate mutual relations when there is no society and no intercourse, and consequently no relations to be regulated.

Secondly, it is necessary that among the members of a society there should be some community of thought and aspiration, though it is, of course, highly desirable that a certain variety of outlook should exist as well. But if ideals and standards are so different that the members practically fail to understand each other, they are quite unable to work together, and it is impossible for them to unite for the accomplishment of common purposes. I remember once declining to join an association of clergy formed to go together in groups on foreign tours. My reason was that a healthy admixture of the lay element was necessary in order to obtain in full measure the recreation, refreshment and instruction we expect from travel abroad. I still think I was right; but if in my ardour for variety of view I had taken the extreme course of joining a club of Publicans and Bar-tenders on a Whitsuntide excursion, I should probably have felt so isolated and uncomfortable that before long I should have deeply regretted my leap from the clerical frying-pan into the Liquor Trade fire! A certain amount of community of interest is requisite for the welfare, and even the existence, of all societies. Exactly how much of it is essential no wise man will venture to define. But we can at any rate declare that social life is impossible when people live on such different planes of thought that they are altogether incapable of seeing and understanding each other's points of view.

All this applies in large measure to states as well as to individuals. The ideas of the most reactionary government in Europe would appear like enlightenment itself when compared with those of a cattle-stealing, man-slaying, witchcraft-loving Central African potentate. The manners and customs, standards and ideals, of Seven Dials or Montmartre would be deemed fastidious and impossible by the dwarfs of the Upper Congo or the Black-Fellows of Central Australia. Such peoples and rulers as these could not be received into the Family of Nations. But when communities are sufficiently civilised to render it possible for their envoys to meet on something like equal terms with those of European and American states, to honour the engagements entered into by their representatives, and to treat with substantial justice subjects of other powers resident among them, then they can be received into international society without danger to its future. They may not at first wield any considerable influence. They may indeed find their privileges somewhat curtailed in comparison with those of older members, as is the case with several Oriental realms who are not allowed full rights of jurisdiction over subjects of Western states resident within their borders. But on the whole it is better for them, and for the rest of the world, to admit them than to keep them outside. International Law, as we shall soon see, sprang up among a group of powers which had been for centuries under the influence of Christianity; and at one time there was a tendency to assert that it was peculiar to Christian states. But this position became impossible with the formal admission of the Mahometan state of Turkey into the Society of Nations by the Treaty of Paris of 1856. At the Hague Conferences of 1899 and 1907 five non-Christian countries—Turkey, Persia, Siam, China and Japan—were seated at the International Council Board. By the latter date one of them, Japan, had won for herself a position among the Great World-Powers to whom the political leadership of civilised humanity is tacitly conceded. The other four were still deprived of full territorial jurisdiction over the inhabitants of Western States resident in their dominions. In other respects they are full subjects of International Law, possessed of all the rights it confers, and subject to all the obligations it imposes. In the modern world civilisation rather than religion has been the passport of admission into the Society of Nations. Whenever a state has been found willing to shape its international action according to the ideas developed originally in Europe and put in practice first among European countries, it has been received by the old-established members of the international family with a welcome corresponding in cordiality to the completeness of its approximation to their standards.

In the third place it is obvious from what has just been set forth that states are regarded as possessors of a definite portion of the earth's surface. In fact the conception of territorial sovereignty is essential. There could be no Society of Nations, and no International Law, without it. Nomadic tribes wandering over a continent, in one place to-day and hundreds of miles away in six months' time, could not develop among themselves any system of regular communication, or establish mutual rights, duties and services. They might now and again meet and fight. Now and again two or three of them might arrange some isolated transaction, such as an exchange of goods or captives, or an alliance for a foray. But anything worthy of the name of Society would be impossible. Communities must settle down on the land before they can maintain with one another regular and continuous intercourse.

We are now in a position to understand that no real International Law is possible unless a considerable number of states, imbued with similar ideas as to society and government, exist together in a world which recognises that dominion over a certain portion of the earth's surface is an essential attribute of statehood. Simple as these conditions appear to us they were not satisfied till a comparatively modern epoch in the history of mankind. There was indeed in ancient Greece some approach to a very rudimentary International code. The little City-States into which the Greek world was divided recognised that in virtue of their common Hellenic descent there was something special between them in the way of mutual rights and duties. This feeling survived the terrible severities of their warfare and the frequent lapses into piracy of some of their communities. It decreed that the persons of heralds and envoys were sacred. Truces and treaties it deemed inviolable. Burial was granted to the dead who fell on the battlefield; and the living were held entitled to freedom from molestation when travelling to and from the chief seats of Hellenic worship. But, as Dr. T. A. Walker has well observed, "The International Law of such a people could hardly, it is clear, be more than an inter-municipal law."[1] Such in fact it was; and the group of municipalities among which it held a somewhat uncertain sway was small when compared with the great world outside. As to the non-Hellenic, the so-called Barbarian peoples, a still more elementary and still less rigidly observed law was recognised as applicable to them. But its obligation was derived more from the general feeling as to what was fitting and honourable than from any notion that

[1] *History of the Law of Nations*, Vol. I, p. 38.

Barbarian peoples had, or could have, any rights against Greek states.

Soon "the glory that was Greece" faded from the earth, and was followed by the dominion of all-conquering Rome. Her Empire in its palmy days almost covered the civilised world. Without were Chimeras dire, and naked savages, and dim realms hidden away beyond the Pillars of Hercules and in the mysterious recesses of the farthest East. Within were not only individual subjects dependent in all things on Roman Law and Roman magistrates, but also kingdoms, districts, cities, retaining greater or less powers of self-government. Disputes between them, or between their subjects and themselves, were referred to Cæsar, where he sat in the Eternal City surrounded by his Jurists, his Generals and his Statesmen. He was supreme judge as well as supreme law-giver, and, as such, dealt with subject rulers and commonwealths as well as private citizens. Before long civilised mankind, generalising from its own experience, developed the idea of universal sovereignty, and held that there was, and ought to be, a power above all other powers, which should in the last resort not only dictate its will to all its immediate subjects, but also control the actions of subordinate rulers. "It is better," said Augustus of the terrible founder of the Herodian line, "to be his pig than his son." But his own permission had to be given before even Herod the Great could execute a prince of the royal house. By means of this supreme authority the fairest and most fertile portions of the earth's surface were kept at peace for many generations; and so great was the boon thus given to men that they saw nothing incongruous in the worship of the Emperor, who summed up in his own person the glory and majesty of a rule which gave security to a grateful world.

In time Christian influences prevailed, and Cæsar was no longer deified. But the triumph of the Cross did much more than abolish sacrifices to dead Emperors. It profoundly modified fundamental political conceptions. Early in the fourth century Constantine the Great made Christianity into the official religion of the Empire; and though the Church lost in consequence much of its pristine zeal and purity, it gradually influenced current nations of government and social order by a long process of peaceful penetration. The idea of universal sovereignty was not weakened thereby but received fresh vigour instead. The fall of the Roman Empire of the West failed to destroy it; and a new life descended upon it when Charlemagne reestablished the Empire under ecclesiastical auspices, and was crowned by the Pope in the Basilica of St. Peter at Rome on Christmas Day, A.D. 800, amid the acclamations of the people, who hailed the Frankish hero as *Augustus* and *Imperator.*

This daring and fruitful deed changed the face of history, and rendered possible the mediæval theory of one great Christendom, the Kingdom of God on earth, governed in temporal matters by the head of the revived or Holy Roman Empire, and in spiritual matters by the Pope as head of the Western Church, which claimed to be at once Catholic and Roman. And as there were two potentates, so there were two swords, the temporal wielded by the Emperor, the spiritual by the Pope. Each was granted by God for the due governance of His baptised people. They formed the great World-State, the one vast realm over which He ruled supreme through His two lieutenants. Pope and Emperor, it was held, exercised authority by divine decree. They were to walk together in righteousness, each attending to his allotted sphere, for the good of Christ's people and the enlargement of His Kingdom on earth. But practice soon fell far short of theory, and before long the usual relation between the two Vicegerents of the Almighty was that of open or veiled hostility. Mediæval history is full of their quarrels, and mediæval literature of the controversies of their partisans. In the heat of the conflict the notion of co-operation on equal terms tended to vanish; and each side claimed supremacy for its chief. But for ages neither imperialist nor papalist denied that universal sovereignty must somewhere be found if right were done in the sphere of government.

At last facts grew too strong for theories that had long ceased to be inductions from them. On a world in which the power of the Emperor had for ages been of little account outside Germany and the hereditary possessions of the House of Hapsburg the storm of the Reformation burst, shattering Papal authority over half Europe far more completely than Imperial authority had been destroyed by a slow process of decay. At the same time the revival of learning revealed again the independent political life of ancient Greece, and created a spirit which strove for the emancipation of the human mind from the shackles of authority. The Reformation and the Renaissance together destroyed the idea of a common superior over states.

The removal of the old restraining influences not only dispersed much moral and intellectual fog, but let loose at first some of the worst elements in human nature. Statecraft became more unscrupulous and war more cruel. As usual the intellectual need of justifying evil practice led to evil theory, and evil theory led in turn to a vast increase of evil practice. Machiavelli, the astute Florentine statesman, separated statecraft from other portions of human conduct, and divorced it entirely from ordinary morality. His famous work *The Prince,* published early in the sixteenth century, would never have been written had not courts and camps been full of anarchial speculations and outrageous acts of perfidy and cruelty. But its great influence and popularity vastly increased the tendency towards lawlessness in international transactions. It taught that the business of a Prince or ruler is first and foremost to maintain his authority and if possible increase his dominions. Accordingly he is "to have no other design, nor thought, nor study, but war and the arts and disciplines of it, for indeed that is the only profession worthy of a Prince, and is of so much importance that it not only preserves those that are born Princes in their patrimonies, but advances men of private condition to that honourable degree."[1] He is "to learn to be good or otherwise according to the exigence of his affairs . . . for if we consider things impartially we shall find some things in appearance are virtuous, and yet, if pursued would bring certain destruction; and others on the contrary are seemingly bad, which, if followed by a Prince, procure his peace and security."[2] As to humanity, "he is not to regard the scandal of being cruel, if thereby he keeps his subjects in their allegiance and united,"[3] while as to good faith he "neither can nor ought to keep his word when to keep it is hurtful, and the causes which led him to pledge it are removed."[4]

Nicolo Machiavelli banished morality from statecraft, and the rough fighting-men among his disciples banished it from war. In neither sphere had it obtained more than a precarious foothold; but things were sadly worsened when it disappeared altogether. The evil culminated a century or more after the death of its chief contriver in the terrible Thirty Years' War. I have given in another place a brief account of the horrors of that awful time, and from it I venture now to take a few descriptive sentences. "Famine and pestilence followed in the wake of the armies. There was no pity, no reverence, no devotion. Wolfish ferocity, blasphemous impiety, unbridled lust, bore sway over the words and deeds of men. Whole dis-

[1] *The Prince,* Ch. XIV.
[2] *Ibid.,* Ch. XV.
[3] *Ibid.,* Ch. XVII.
[4] *Ibid.,* Ch. XVIII.

tricts went out of cultivation, and were restored to forest and wilderness. The wretched inhabitants, such of them as were left alive, formed predatory bands, and lived by robbery. Often the gibbets were deprived of their ghastly load to satisfy the pangs of hunger. But cannibalism was frequently preceded by murder. Human beings, turned by misery into wild beasts, rivalled the beasts in ferocity and foulness. Greed was rampant, and nothing was secure from the spoiler. Even the abodes of the dead were ransacked in the search for treasure, and the mouldering bodies thrown out to the kites and the wolves. Men gloried in their wickedness. They chanted litanies of the devil, they sang songs in praise of lust and torture, they raged with special fury against churches, priests and pastors. In the remote country districts religion died; and learning perished from the Universities."[1] At the end of the struggle in 1648 whole provinces were depopulated; and even at the beginning Hugo Grotius, the great father of the Law of Nations, was impelled to write the oft-quoted words, "I saw prevailing throughout the Christian world a licence in making war of which even barbarous nations would have been ashamed, recourse being had to arms for slight reasons and no reason; and when arms were once taken up all reverence for human and divine law was thrown away, just as if men were henceforth authorised to commit all crimes without restraint."[2]

[1] Lawrence, *Essays*, p. 181.

[2] *De Jure Belli ac Pacis*, Prolegomena, § 28.

Into such a world as this modern International Law was born. Blood-stained and dishonourable as were its surroundings, in some respects the times were favourable. The disappearance of the notion of a common superior ruling over one great composite Christian realm left the field clear for the idea of a Society of independent states. The theory that sovereignty was not universal but territorial, due probably at first to feudalism but destined to survive its origin, gave a legal basis to the claims of Kings and other potentates. For were they not as against each other proprietors of the lands they governed and was not supreme rule associated with ownership of a portion of the earth's surface? Above all the crying need of something to take the place of the old discarded restraints and save the world from moral anarchy disposed men to try new projects, if only they promised to curb the unbridled ambitions of princes, and the ferocious cruelty of armies. Thus it was that we got back again in the first half of the seventeenth century to a Society of Nations, but a Society very different from the group of City-States we saw in ancient Greece. It was a Society permeated through and through by Christian influences and endowed with a great heritage of Greek Philosophy and Roman Law. Moreover, though it was cruel and barbarous in many of its usages, it arose among peoples accustomed for centuries to the idea that order and government were normal incidents of human life. The modern state, with no earthly authority over it, had arrived. How was it to act when faced by its fellows on the world-stage opening out before them?

Before we attempt to answer this question it will be worth while to pause a moment and consider whether progressive Christian civilisation is not in as great danger now as it was in the days of Tilly, and Mansfeld, and Wallenstein, and Christian of Brunswick. We have just described the result of the principles of Machiavelli applied in the field as well as in the cabinet. Surely a similar cause is producing similar effects at the present time. The seed has been sown far more diligently in Germany than anywhere else;[1] but the harvest is being garnered all over the world. The historical theories of Treitschke, with his worship of power stored up in the autocratic state, the sociological theories of Bernhardi, with his loudly proclaimed belief in the necessity and inherent nobility of war, have not even the merit of originality. They are merely disguised Machiavellianism, with a dash of imperfectly understood Biology thrown in. And they are rapidly repeating in the world the evil work that was done by their predecessors three hundred years ago. On the German side in the present war bad faith has again been justified by state necessity. Great International Treatieshave been torn asunder as mere scraps of paper whenever it is deemed that state policy can be furthered thereby or military advantages secured. Further we have seen a terrible recrudescence of inhuman barbarities as far as the incidents of actual warfare are

[1] F. Von Hügel, *The German Soul*, pp. 132-145.

concerned. We have not yet perhaps got so far as cannibalism, though even with regard to this crowning horror it would not be wise to hazard a too emphatic negative, seeing that in Poland, and Serbia, and Armenia, people are known to have perished in thousands of hunger, and in such a dire strait human nature may sometimes revert to primitive ferocity. But undoubtedly German troops have of set purpose, and not in fits of temporary madness, desecrated graves, violated women, and mutilated children. Unarmed civilians have been used as screens for advancing columns. Food supplies have been torn from starving populations. Prisoners of war have perished by thousands of privation, and many more have been done to death by persistent and calculated cruelty. In some districts men and women have been taken from their homes by German invaders, and made to labour on military works devised for the destruction of their own countrymen. This is little better than a return to the slavery which was of old the fate of the inhabitants of conquered territory. And Teutonic ingenuity is equal to the task of devising new barbarities as well as reviving old ones. It has taken the triumphs of modern science, and prostituted them to the service of unsoldierly brutality. New gases have been invented to kill the enemy wholesale by slow torture, new chemical compounds to burn him to death. Not long before the war man achieved the conquest of the air, and the first use to which Germany put this fresh victory of the human mind was to rain down explosive bombs and fire-raising projectiles on the civilian population of enemy cities, and even on dressing stations and hospitals. At much the same time the discovery was made that the depths of the sea could be safely traversed by craft specially constructed for the purpose. Immediately German submarines attacked enemy merchantmen as well as enemy warships, and sometimes sent to the bottom without warning the unarmed voyagers upon them. In several conspicuous instances helpless women and children were thus destroyed, either at once by drowning or, after long hours of exposure in open boats, by cold and exhaustion. But such horrors were only a beginning. Worse followed afterwards. In certain wide stretches of water neutral vessels were attacked as well as belligerents; and by and by the sanctity of the sick and wounded was violated by the torpedoing of Hospital Ships and the slaughter of Nurses and Doctors. For this no sudden outbreak of passionate hate is responsible, but cold-blooded and deliberate iniquity. Those who are familiar with the majestic verse of Milton will remember how, in the Council of the rebel angels after the first day of the great battle in heaven, Satan himself demonstrated the ease with which tubes and projectiles could be made that

> shall send forth
> From far, with thundering noise, among our foes,
> Such implements of mischief as shall dash
> To pieces and o'erwhelm whatever stands
> Adverse.[1]

And then the poet goes on to describe how the advice of

[1] *Paradise Lost,* Bk. VI.

the enemy of mankind was taken by his followers; and how the terrible enginery

> Secret they finished, and in order set
> With silent circumspection, unespied.[1]

May we not trace to some such infernal origin what the German High Command euphemistically calls the unrestricted U-boat warfare of its submarines?

Enough has been said to shew the similarity between the present crisis and the great outburst of lawlessness in international affairs three centuries ago. The two are alike in the theories that gave rise to them, and in the unutterable miseries which accompanied the translation of those theories into practice. On the first occasion a great moral and intellectual revolt against Machiavellianism stayed, if it did not stamp out, the plague. It behoves us to study this movement carefully with a view to finding out whether some further development of it may not be able to check the present evil.

The answer to the question how the modern state was to act towards its fellows when the inexorable logic of events had substituted a number of independent sovereignties for one world-wide realm could not of course be reached as the result of a process of pure reasoning. The past had to be taken into account. In the sixteenth and seventeenth centuries the world was not, any more than it is now, a blank sheet of paper on which some all-powerful and influential personage could write

[1] *Paradise Lost,* Bk. VI.

what characters he pleased. If the law of the beast, the philosophy of the tiger-spring and the pig-sty, was not to prevail to the utter undoing of civilisation and humanity, it was necessary to search the mental and moral heritage of the age for elements that were capable of being built up into a new and better international order. A succession of great writers found and utilised such elements, all of which, it is worthy of note, had one feature in common. They were held to be universal in their application and binding by reason of their inherent worth, without regard to any force that could be invoked to compel obedience to them. Whether this was true we need not stop to discuss. The important point is that in the last half of the sixteenth century and the first half of the seventeenth century the vast majority of thinkers in every European country believed it to be true. The elements in question were Roman Law, Canon Law, International Custom, and Christian Morality. We will take them separately, and give a brief account of each as a factor in the creation and development of the modern Law of Nations.

1. The first to be considered is *Roman Law*. Many of us have remembered from our school days the ringing lines in which Macaulay describes the great work of ancient Rome as conquest and dominion,

> Thine, Roman, is the pilum;
> Roman! the sword is thine;
> The even trench, the bristling mound,
> The legion's ordered line.

But the great historian might have added, though he did not, that after all the chief gift of the eternal city to humanity was not military science, but law. He might have sung, though he did not,

> Thine, Roman, is the jurist,
> Roman! the code is thine;
> The sentence deep, the reasoned rule,
> The judgment's ordered line.

Taking its rise in the customs of a few semi-barbarous tribes, Roman Law gradually developed into a great scientific system. Consolidated early in the sixth century by Justinian, or rather by the Jurists he gathered together for the purpose, it stood, under the name of the *Corpus Juris Civilis,* as the acknowledged law of the Eastern Empire, till Constantinople fell before the onslaught of Mahomet II in 1453. In the West after Rome's downfall from her high estate it remained the heritage of the Roman populations under their barbarian masters. And when a man of insight as well as courage was at the head of a horde of semi-savage invaders it formed the chief material of the code he strove to impose on his followers. As new political arrangements grew up amidst the ruins of the Roman Empire of the West the study of Roman Law revived in the Universities that arose during the twelfth and thirteenth centuries. At Bologna, at Paris, and at Oxford and other seats of learning, Professors lectured on the *Corpus Juris Civilis.* It was the great *litera scripta* of an age when an almost superstitious reverence was felt for the written word, and in many spheres its authority remained unchallenged in spite of the growth of homespun national laws. Right up to the end of the sixteenth century it was deemed to have a special and direct bearing on disputes between heads of states. Accordingly the founders of modern International Law drew on it for many of the rules they laid down. The Civilians, as its teachers were called, kept alive the idea of a science of law in the midst of the chaotic masses of local custom out of which national laws emerged. There is hardly a legal system in the civilised world which has not been influenced to a greater or less degree by the majestic jurisprudence of Imperial Rome.

2. *Canon Law* demands our attention next. It was based on the *Jus Civile* to a large extent, and was always studied in close connection with it. Side by side with the Civilian in mediæval Universities stood the Canonist, and in the great system of Ecclesiastical Courts which culminated in the Roman Curia he held undisputed sway. The law he studied and developed transcended, like the Civil Law, all national boundaries. It held good from one end of Christendom to the other, and was administered by those Courts Christian which were so often in violent conflict with National and Royal Courts. It was a digest of the canons of Church Councils and decrees of Popes eked out by quotations from the writings of ecclesiastics of accepted authority and a certain number of texts from the *Corpus Juris Civilis*. This latter was indeed its model as to form;

and at last in 1580 Pope Gregory XIII set forth a *Corpus Juris Canonici* in imitation of the earlier code. When it became necessary to find rules and principles for the conduct of international affairs, the first writers who attempted the task made frequent use of the various digests and collections of the Canon Law of Western Christendom.

3. *The Customs of States in their dealings one with another.*

Clearly if a Society is to subsist at all in the absence of a common superior to dictate its laws it must fall back on rules of conduct obeyed by its members because they think fit to observe them. That is to say it must be guided to a large extent by custom. But customs are good, bad and indifferent. With regard to the last, the indifferent in point of goodness or badness, usage is its own justification. There is, for instance, no special ground in reason and morality why a gentleman should salute the ladies of his acquaintance by taking off his hat to them when he meets them in the street. Any other form of courtesy would do as well. This particular form however happens to be prescribed by a custom which has sprung up, no one knows how, in decent society, and so we all follow it. Similar instances can be quoted from the intercourse of nations. Usage goes so far as to prescribe the size of the paper by means of which communications of various kinds pass from one state to another. It does even more. It settles the exact kind of communication that a self-respecting Foreign Office should send on gold-edged sheets.[1] Far be it from me to belittle the importance of these observances. Yet I venture to suggest that though we may safely leave them as they are, no great harm would be done if they were otherwise. But when matters that involve right and wrong are concerned, customs must be weighed in the balance and judged. That a rule has been followed in the past is not sufficient justification for continuing to follow it in the future. The question of the proper tests to apply and the proper method of their application must be reserved for the present, except in so far as it is dealt with under the next head. I hope to discuss it in the second lecture.

4. *Christian Morality.*

Appeals were constantly made by the great writers who founded modern International Law to Christian rules of life, even as against customs which they admitted to be so general among the most civilised states of the time that it was impossible to refuse them admission into the international code. This is particularly the case as regards war. Its usages are necessarily harsh; and those who generalised from the practice of antiquity had to admit that it allowed the general slaughter of all enemy subjects. But they strove to exempt women, children, ministers of religion, and captives as protected by natural feelings of humanity, and even husbandmen, merchants, and workmen, as

[1] Satow, *Guide to Diplomatic Practice,* Vol. I, pp. 85-98.

excepted by the Canons of the Church. In the same spirit they dealt with other portions of the field, striving everywhere to introduce restraints deduced from Christian principles.

Having considered separately the various elements utilised for their purpose by the early writers on International Law, we must now turn to these writers themselves; and though we cannot deal with all of them, there are three who must be selected for brief notice. They are:—

Francis Suarez (1548-1617), a Jesuit theologian and Professor in the University of Coimbra. He published there in 1612 his *Tractatus de Legibus,* in which, as Professor Westlake has said, he "has put on record with a master's hand the existence of a necessary human society transcending the boundaries of states, the indispensableness of rules for that society, the insufficiency of reason to provide with demonstrative force all the rules required, and the right of human society to supply the deficiency by custom enforced as law, such custom being suitable to nature."[1] It is just as well for us, among whom a tendency to disparage the Latin races, the Roman Church, and the religious orders, has been by no means unknown, to note that it is to one who was at once a Spaniard, a Schoolman, a Theologian and a Jesuit, that we owe the clear enunciation of two most fruitful principles. The first is that there is really and truly a Society or Family of Nations, and the second is that the law which must be applied

[1] *Chapters on the Principles of International Law,* pp. 27, 28.

to this family or society is not so much a law *common* to all nations, as the classical Roman Jurist conceived of the *Jus Gentium,* but a law *between* nations, a law which, as Suarez himself says, all peoples and nations ought to observe between themselves. Next in order we must deal with a very different man,

Albericus Gentilis (1552-1608), who was born a few years after Suarez, but died a few years before him. He was an Italian by birth, and at the age of 20 graduated as a doctor of Civil Law in the University of Perugia. There he and his father seem gradually to have adopted heretical Protestant opinions, in consequence of which they had to fly from their native country. We find Albericus first in Austria and afterwards in England. By 1580 he had settled in Oxford, and seems to have enjoyed a career of unabated honour and prosperity there till the end of his life. He was fortunate in securing the patronage of Queen Elizabeth's friend, the Earl of Leicester, who was Chancellor of the University at the time, and got his client made Regius Professor of Civil Law in 1587, the year before the Spanish Armada. Nearly two centuries afterwards he was equally fortunate in obtaining for admirer, editor and biographer, another distinguished son of Oxford in the person of Professor Sir T. E. Holland, who published in 1877 a valuable edition of the *De Jure Belli* of Gentilis. The work is one of several, all dealing with matters that arise out of the intercourse of nations, and all distinguished by a grasp of sound practical considerations rather than philosophical discussion of first principles. He does of course mention Natural Reason and Natural Law, and when met by the obvious consideration that men have differed greatly as to what these command, he declares that mathematical proofs are impossible, and proceeds to deal with historical and legal precedents. In fact, Italian though he was, he had a thoroughly English mind. What has been called the pure ether of speculation had no attractions for him. He is always the well-informed practical man, on whom his learning sits lightly, but who brings an acute mind and a sound judgment to the discussion of questions vitally important at the moment. His great strength lay in arrangement and the skill with which he disentangled his arguments from irrelevant matter, going straight to the heart of the question under discussion. To his treatise on the Law of War Grotius owed much of the plan and a good deal of the subject-matter of his own immortal work. We pass now to an account, necessarily very brief, of the life and labour of this greatest of all the founders of the modern Law of Nations.

Hugo Grotius (1583-1645), "the miracle of Holland," as he was called by Henry IV of France, was attached at the age of 15 to the embassy of John of Barneveld to that monarch. The year before he had taken his Bachelor's degree at the University of Leyden, which had been founded in 1575 in memory of the siege and the great deliverance of the previous year. As a student he must often have wandered over the country then occupied by the Spanish lines, and gazed from the ramparts at the fields which had been restored to the waves in order that Boisot and his Zealanders might sail over them to the relief of the famine-stricken city. He became a marvel of erudition, while his training in practical affairs kept him from pedantry. He was at once a great scholar, a great theologian, a great lawyer, an acute diplomatist, an able historian, and a melodious poet. It is impossible here to give a biography of him. All that can be done is to mention a few facts in a great career. At the age of 17 he commenced practice at the bar. At 24 he was made Advocator-General of Holland. In 1607 he published his *Mare Liberum* in favour of the doctrine that the high seas are free from territorial sovereignty. In 1608 he married. He took the Arminian and State Rights side in the religious and political controversy that convulsed the newly-founded Republic of the United Netherlands, and in 1618 was condemned in consequence to perpetual imprisonment. But in 1621 he was enabled through the devotion of his wife to escape from the castle where he was confined. The imprisoned statesman was tall and handsome, but he managed to squeeze himself into a trunk about 4 feet long, which was supposed to contain the books he had borrowed from his friends. His wife turned the key, kissed the lock, and sent for the soldiers who were to carry the trunk out of the castle and take it to the house of a friend in Gorcum, the nearest town. As they lifted it, one of them said, " The Arminian himself must be in it, it is so heavy." " Not the Arminian," replied Madam Grotius, " only heavy Arminian books." Just outside the castle a soldier declared he would get a gimlet and bore a hole into the Arminian. "Then," said a maidservant who had accompanied the precious chest, " you must get a gimlet that will reach to the top of the castle where the Arminian lies abed and asleep." At last the box reached its destination, and Grotius stepped out among his friends, pale and faint, but nevertheless full of life and resource. He was at once disguised as a bricklayer, and taken out of the town. After many adventures he reached Paris, and resided there till 1631, living with difficulty on a pension granted him by the French King and very irregularly paid. In 1625 he published his most celebrated book, the *De Jure Belli ac Pacis*. In 1635 he entered into the service of Queen Christina of Sweden as her Ambassador to France, and died in 1645 at Rostock from the effects of a shipwreck which befel him on a voyage from Stockholm. Thus sadly ended a great life. The most marvellous thing connected with it was the wonderful success of the *De Jure Belli ac Pacis*. At first it sold very slowly; but within a few years it was taught as Public Law in the Universities of Heidelberg and Wittenberg. Gustavus Adolphus carried a copy about with him on his campaigns, and, it is said, always slept with it under his pillow. In 1648 its leading principles were acted on in the Peace of Westphalia, which put an end to the mediæval theory of international relations, and inaugurated the modern state-system. Thus within a generation of its publication by a poor and exiled scholar it had profoundly modified the thought of the world, and moulded the rising Society of Nations.

This Society was then in a condition we find it very hard to picture to ourselves. It included about 2000 separate sovereignties, most of them insignificant in size and importance. And yet this numerous body did not cover the whole geographical area of Europe, to say nothing of lands beyond the European borders. Russia was outside it and remained outside till the masterful genius of Peter the Great forced for her an entrance into the councils and alliances of her Western neighbours. Turkey, proud of the terror she inspired as the scourge of Christendom, held haughtily aloof from the company of states she despised as infidel, and proclaimed aloud her freedom from the rules they imposed on themselves for the conduct of their mutual intercourse. The new Society of Nations, though as regards the number of its members large, and indeed too large for real association, was, as regards the area of territory within its limits, small in comparison with the world outside. The gradual transformation of this Europe into the Europe of the days just before the great World-War will be traced in the next two lectures.

LECTURE II.

THE GROWTH OF INTERNATIONAL SOCIETY.

At the end of the previous lecture we took a necessarily hurried survey of the European State-System as it existed during the middle of the seventeenth century. The Peace of Westphalia which laid the foundation of the new order established the principle of territorial sovereignty as part of the public law of the civilised world. It did this in effect when it recognised the complete independence of sovereign states, and confined the real power of the Emperor to dominion over the hereditary possessions of the House of Hapsburg. His shadowy headship of a loose German Confederation barely obscured the fact that its leading states were in the habit of ignoring or flouting his authority, and even its lesser members were constantly entering into combinations and counter-combinations with little regard to his interests, and without troubling to ask of him leave or licence. We also saw that the Family of Nations, though unlike other families it began by being very large, did not cover in extent of territory an area nearly as great as the realms beyond its borders.

But since 1648 enormous alterations have taken

place. Two great processes have been going on continuously and simultaneously. A vast crowd of wholly artificial international atoms situated mainly but by no means exclusively in Germany have disappeared through absorption in larger realms. The startling result is that instead of the two thousand or so international units existing in Europe when Grotius wrote, we have now only twenty-two, if we leave out as separate states the twenty-four members of the Federal Union commonly called the German Empire, seeing that they can have little or no foreign policy apart from it. The Society of Nations has thus been simplified from within to an absolutely enormous extent.

At the same time it has been amplified from without in an equally amazing manner. No one dreamed in 1648 that the vast colonial possessions of Spain in South and Central America would become independent states in less than two hundred years. Nor, when Virginia was founded in 1607 as the first English colony on the mainland of the American continent, would anyone have predicted that it, and twelve other colonies, none of which were then in existence, would before the end of the next century throw off the dominion of the British Crown, and by rapid growth in extent and power become in a short time, as a Federal Republic, a highly influential factor in international relations. Throughout the last century the weight of the New World in the councils of the powers steadily increased, and in 1907 at the second Hague Conference no less than nineteen states from North, Central and

South America were present by their representatives and took their full share in the proceedings.

The New World drew its civilisation from the Old, and therefore it had no difficulty in assimilating rules of international intercourse which had grown up originally among the nations of Europe. We find its statesmen quoting from the beginning opinions of European authorities on the *Jus Gentium* and referring in international controversies to precedents drawn from European history. When the United States, Chili, Peru and the rest started on their separate national careers, they became at the same time members of the Society of Nations and subjects of International Law. There was no question, as there was with the independent realms of Asia, of formal admission or admission on condition that the full rights of territorial jurisdiction over resident foreigners were curtailed in the interest of the subjects of Western powers. The newcomers entered the august company of civilised states on equal terms with the rest, and though the warnings given by Washington in his Farewell Address against entanglement in "the ordinary combinations and collisions" of the European state system have been sometimes quoted in favour of the complete political isolation of the New World, the sound sense of American statesmen has prevented any serious attempt to create two Societies of Nations and two systems of International Law. The famous Monroe Doctrine, enunciated by the President of that name in his December Message of 1823, aimed at nothing more than the preservation of the American continent for the American peoples. It inaugurated no attempt to build a Chinese Wall of exclusion round the rising states of the New World, and thus cut them off from dangerous European influences. "Cultivate peace and harmony with all" wrote the great Father of his country, and the statesmen who succeeded him held themselves bound to put in practice this part of his political testament as well as the other. Indeed the Monroe Doctrine itself is a proof of their solicitude as to both. Its enunciation was preceded, and to some extent caused, by negotiations in which England, France, Russia and Spain were concerned. To George Canning, the brilliant Foreign Secretary of Great Britain, the Message of President Monroe brought great joy. Its uncompromising declaration against possible interference on the part of the Holy Alliance with the revolted South and Central American Republics which had declared their independence of Spain, came as a most welcome aid in his diplomatic struggle with the forces of militant despotism in Europe.

Europe on its part never attempted to exclude the American Republics from the Society of Nations, or bade them withdraw and start a separate society of their own. Even in those early days of which we have been speaking their commercial and social ties with the Old World, their community of religion and culture, and their recognition of the sacred claims of humanity, prevented anything of the kind. And the recent action of President Wilson and the United States Congress in joining the great Confederation against aggressive and autocratic Germany has been received by the free peoples of Europe so joyfully and enthusiastically as to make it clear that no severance between the two groups of states will be contemplated in future. Civilised humanity must hold together if it is to work out its own salvation. It must learn to put down wanton disturbers of the peace, punish deliberate violations of good faith and humanity, and lead the backward races along the paths of progress. For these purposes it needs the counsel and strength of all the nations which compose it. No one has set forth this noble idea more forcibly in the midst of a world orgy of destruction and bloodshed than the present Chief Magistrate of the United States. To no one do we look with more confidence for wise and valiant efforts to realise it when peace returns. The formation of the Pan-American Union in recent times is quite consistent with it. The object of the Union is the bringing together of all the independent states of North and South America for the development of their natural resources, and the strengthening of the spiritual bonds between their peoples. These things may be done without any disregard of the welfare of the world at large. They may instead help it forward in no small degree.

We are now able to lay down with confidence the proposition that the period between the age of Grotius and the outbreak of the present war has seen the gathering together into one great Society of all states with any pretensions to advanced civilisation. This

Society arose at first among the Christian nations of Europe. It developed internally by simplification, which greatly reduced the original number of its members while it turned them into a somewhat loosely organised body of international units. At the same time it developed externally by amplification till it embraced all the independent states of Europe and North and South America, and most of the independent states of Asia. Even this is not all, for in reality it covers the greater part of the land-area of the globe. The states possessed of colonies and dependencies, protectorates and spheres of influence, speak for them in international intercourse. At international conferences the voice of Great Britain, for instance, is really the voice of the whole British Empire, including India and the self-governing Dominions. In the same way the voice of France is really the voice of all the French possessions, including Algeria in Africa and Indo-China in Asia, while the United States of America represents Hawaii, the Philippine Islands and Porto Rico, as well as its continental domains. Thus nearly the whole world is taken into account when all its civilised states meet, as they have done once in history at the Hague Conference of 1907 and may do often again. It is quite true that at The Hague the representation was crude and unsatisfactory, the methods of discussion confused, and the means for giving practical effect to the decisions reached lamentably inefficient. But in process of time remedies may be found for these crying evils. Meanwhile a very great thing—one of the greatest things in all history—has come to pass. Civilised humanity has met, and endeavoured to act in concert for the common good.

The world-wide Society of which we have been speaking has its grades like other social bodies. We will not stop to speak here of the differences between sovereign and part-sovereign, neutralised and non-neutralised states. They are too technical for our present purpose; but there is one distinction so important that it cannot be passed over. I refer to the separation between the Great Powers and the other members of the Family of Nations. It is a distinction based rather upon differences of position and influence than differences of legal rights. The Great Powers are those which by reason of their strength and size and activity have a preponderant voice in the conclaves of the nations. If they are agreed, other states find it difficult to say them nay. The leadership of the Society of Nations is tacitly conceded to them; and they admit others into their body from time to time by a sort of common impulse, springing from a regard to obvious facts. The system arose in Europe, but has recently spread beyond its boundaries as International Society itself ceased to be European only and became world-wide. The number of Great Powers has varied from time to time. The international settlement which followed the downfall of Napoleon made them five—England, France, Austria, Prussia and Russia. These were called the five Great Powers of Europe; and five they remained all through the middle period of the nineteenth century. The consolidation of Italy into one Kingdom under the House of Savoy brought a fresh element within the European equilibrium. Note was taken of this new fact when in 1867 the Great Powers invited her to join them at the Conference of London, which settled for the time the dangerous Luxemburg question by neutralising the Grand Duchy. This invitation raised the new Kingdom to the rank of a Great Power, and from that time there were six of them instead of five. But soon the growing wealth and population of the United States, and the commercial and humanitarian interests which forced it almost against its will to take part in the settlement of momentous questions which arose outside the two Americas, caused it to be regarded as a Great Power. An American representative attended the Congo Conference of 1884-1885 and signed its Final Act, which opened up the vast interior of the African Continent to the enterprise of the civilised world, settled to some extent the distribution of territory within it, and made war upon the Liquor Traffic with the natives and the more infamous Slave Trade. A little later, American plenipotentiaries took a prominent and beneficent part in both the Hague Conferences and also in the Algeciras Conference of 1906 which warded off for a time the danger of European War over the Morocco question.

But this is not all. As the Society of Nations extended over the world, its inner circle was enlarged by the admission of the new elements. We have just seen how the United States entered the ranks of the

Great Powers from America. Soon Asia supplied a further reinforcement in the person of Japan. This happened in 1907 when the second Hague Conference was engaged in an attempt to create an International Prize Court of Appeal. It was then decided that eight states should always have a representative judge among the fifteen who were to form the court, the seven other judges being assigned to the remaining thirty-six states by rota. The states thus singled out from the rest were Great Britain, France, Austria, Germany, Italy, Russia, the United States and Japan, which last was thus raised to the rank of a Great Power. At present, therefore, there are eight of them, and they are no longer Great Powers of Europe, but Great World-Powers. To-day it is parochial to think in continents. We have now to consider the whole globe. Moreover, there is nothing mystic or final in the number eight. Doubtless other states may from time to time be added to the group of Great Powers, and it is possible that some may drop out of it. In the Society of Nations as well as in the society of individuals, a process of ebb and flow is constantly going on, and a state like a human being may fall from a position of consideration and leadership.[1] Indeed it is by no means certain that what may be called the collective hegemony of the Great Powers will prove more than a passing phenomenon. In the reconstruction of International Society that must be effected after the present war it may vanish alto-

[1] The position of Austria at the present moment (Nov., 1918) is a case in point.

gether. But on the other hand it may develop in an altered and improved form into a means of entrusting to a body representative of the whole of civilised humanity the all-important task of making peacefully such changes in the international order as may be required from time to time. Questions such as this I hope to discuss in the last two lectures. I merely refer to it now to shew the possibilities that may lurk in that distinction between the Great Powers and ordinary states which I have been compelled to describe as a fact of present-day international life.

Having noted the chief stages of the development of the Society of Nations in form and extent since the Peace of Westphalia, we must now attempt to trace the growth of the influences which moulded its ideas and shaped the rules which arose from them. We have seen that Grotius and his predecessors convinced the world of the existence of a real Society of Nations, which instead of being lawless and abominable was subject to rules which could be made approximately just and righteous even in the midst of war. We have also tried to discover to what sources they looked for these rules, and have found that one of the chief was the customs followed by states in their mutual intercourse. But here comes in a great difficulty. By what process was it possible to sift good customs from bad, and enable mankind to distinguish between those that were to be followed and those that were to be reprobated? And behind this problem lurked another which jurists call the question of sanction. How, that is to say, can rules, when made, be enforced in cases where they are not obeyed willingly because of a conscientious belief in their goodness and usefulness? This matter cannot be discussed at present, though I hope to deal with it at some length before the course is over. But the former must be touched on here; and I will endeavour to clear it as far as possible from mere technicalities, and concentrate attention on a few essential points.

Grotius believed in a Natural Law, which he based on what he called "the rational and social nature of man" [1] and used as a touchstone to distinguish between what was to be followed and what was to be avoided in the intercourse of human beings. Natural reason, he declared, dictated certain rules which were so sacred and immutable that even the Almighty could not alter them. They were part of the very nature and essence of things, and God Himself submitted to be judged by them.[2] They bound states as well as individuals, and were the fundamental basis of International Law. But beyond them were rules that could be traced to general consent alone, "for what cannot be deduced from certain principles by solid reasoning, and yet is seen and observed everywhere must have its origin from the will and consent of all." [3] Here Grotius seems to have remembered that general consent might be used to justify practices which neither Christianity nor enlight-

[1] *De Jure Belli ac Pacis,* Bk. I, Ch. I, § 12.
[2] *Ibid.,* Bk. I, Ch. I, § 10.
[3] *Ibid.,* Prolegomena, § 40.

ened reason could approve. Accordingly a little further on he qualifies his appeal to the consent of *all* nations by adding " at least the more civilised," and quotes with approval those who " agree that the more savage nations are of less weight in such an estimate." [1] In fact while reading his pages one is never quite sure whether he relies most on his Consent of Nations or on his Natural Law. Still both are there most unmistakably; and he uses all the resources of a vast, though uncritical, erudition to prove his general consent by quotations from writers of all sorts, opinions of statesmen, and declarations of military commanders.

We must now turn to the successors of Grotius, and see how they built up the edifice he and his forerunners had founded. In this connection we will deal in the first place with the Philosophical Jurists, or rather a few of the most important among them. The place of honour next to Grotius must be given to Samuel Pufendorf. He was a native of Chemnitz in Saxony, and became Professor at Heidelberg in 1661. It was there he developed the ideas afterwards embodied in his great work *De Jure Naturæ et Gentium,* published in 1672 at Lund in Sweden, whither its author had removed two years before. He remained, however, in close touch with Germany throughout his life, and died at Berlin in 1694. He differed from Grotius in dispensing entirely with custom as a source of International Law. Not only did he boldly proclaim the all-sufficiency of the so-called Law of Nature, but he

[1] *De Jure Belli ac Pacis,* Bk. I, Ch. I; § 12.

connected it inseparably with a mythical State of Nature, in the existence of which there is no evidence to show that Grotius had the slightest belief. The great Dutchman ignores it. The great German makes it the cornerstone of his philosophical system. He took the notion from Thomas Hobbes of Malmesbury, the great English Political Philosopher of the middle of the seventeenth century. It assumed that there was a time when each individual man ran wild in the woods, doing what was right in his own eyes, free from authority of any kind, and absolutely ignorant of social restraints. Placed thus alone in an almost empty world, the noble savage guided his conduct by the light of his natural reason, and by that alone. Anything less like what we now know to have been the condition of primitive man it is impossible to conceive. But most of the thinkers of the period devoutly believed in it, and attributed to the beings they had divested of all restraints, ideas that could come only from long centuries of social discipline. For instance, it is always assumed that men in a State of Nature attached the highest importance to promises, and kept them with scrupulous good faith, whereas in reality the notion of contract with its mutual obligations is a late growth of fairly advanced civilisation. Ask any traveller who has had the experience of wrestling with native carriers in the forests of Central Africa what sort of appreciation unsophisticated savages have of the sanctity of the plighted word, and you will receive an answer more vigorous than complimentary to his black brethren. But, though the existence of a State of Nature was accepted in most quarters as an axiom of all reasoning about the origin of government, its characteristic features differed according to the cast of thought of the writers who described them. Thus Hobbes held that it was a state of constant war of each against all. The evils of incessant conflict were so terrible that at last human beings met and established by mutual consent states and governments. Pufendorf, on the other hand, declared that primitive man was a social animal who strove to live in amity with his fellows, and agreed to establish rule and authority for the safeguarding of the common weal. In his great work he dealt first with individual conduct and the mutual rights and duties of rulers and ruled, and then towards the end turned to the task of prescribing rules for states in their intercourse with each other. As he had already established to his own satisfaction the existence of a State of Nature, this final step was easy. Since states had no common superior they were related to one another as individuals were before civil authority was established over them, and accordingly they too were under the Law of Nature. Grotius had written concerning the Law of War and Peace. Pufendorf wrote concerning the Law of Nature and Nations. To him the Law of Nations was nothing but the Law of Nature applied to nations; and to nations he attributed a personality and a will analogous to those of individuals.

This was one of the legacies left by the philosopher of Heidelberg to the jurists who came after him. His

Law of Nature, considered as actual law and not as an ideal to which law should ever reach forward, has long ago been relegated to the limbo of discarded theories. His State of Nature collapsed into dust at the first onset of the Historical School. But by insisting on the personality of states he did much to familiarise thinkers with the idea that civilised political units constitute a great family, the members of which flourish by performing brotherly acts towards each other, and contributing according to their power to the common good. This truly Christian idea seems at first sight so obviously right that it cannot be contested. But a little observation shows that it has still to fight its own way against the old, barbaric, and anti-human notion that states can flourish only at the expense of other states, and consequently their first duty is to strengthen themselves at all points in order that they may grab as much as possible of the good things of the world, and hold what they have succeeded in seizing against the attacks of those who are ready to snatch it from them.[1] In the age-long struggle between the international theory of the family and the international theory of the pig-sty, Pufendorf is one of the forces that make for righteousness. So strong was his sense of the sacred ties of our common humanity that he maintained what in his day was the startling proposition that all peoples, and not Christian peoples only, were included within the purview of the Law of Nations.

For a time the system of Pufendorf held the field

[1] F. Naumann, *Briefe über Religion,* 5th ed., pp. 68-87.

in Germany, and was received with favour and deference elsewhere. But by the middle of the eighteenth century a partial reversion to Grotian methods set in under the influence of Christian Wolff, the uncrowned King of German philosophy in the generation before Kant. He attempted in 1749 a study of our subject by what he called a scientific method, which distinguished between a natural law of nations, and a law which arose from voluntary agreement and custom, both being necessary for a complete presentation of the subject. He is now almost forgotten; but in his time he had a great vogue, and made his mark on the development of International Law, partly by recalling attention to those customary rules which Grotius had appealed to and Pufendorf decried, and partly by his own particular doctrine of the inherent rights of states. Moreover, he accentuated, and at the same time exaggerated, the wholesome idea of a Society or Family of Nations, by maintaining that just as individual citizens make up the state, so the whole body of states make up a *civitas maxima,* a sort of superstate of which all are members, and in which they have rights to enjoy and duties to perform. No such world-state existed in his time; but in the midst of the most awful war that ever devastated humanity we have begun to feel acutely the need of some authority in the Society of Nations, which shall secure obedience to its laws and provide for new needs as they arise. I will not anticipate here what I shall have to enlarge upon later in this course, but I may say at once that there are signs of the development in the international body of organs fitted to satisfy its most crying needs, and that the settlement which must follow the present war should, if we are true to our highest aims, show marked progress in this direction. Time may thus vindicate Wolff's insight into tendencies hidden from his fellows. He may pass muster as a prophet, though as a recorder of historic fact he was entirely wrong.

It may be said with truth that the writers we have been discussing were moralists and scholars first and foremost, and only statesmen or lawyers afterwards, if at all. But it would be wrong to deny their usefulness on that account. As thinkers they gave to International Law a philosophic basis which secured for it the respect of an age when all who troubled to reason about the problems of society and government believed in Nature and her Law. It was no slight achievement to convince the world that this exalted, if somewhat obscure and mysterious code, laid down just and humane rules for the guidance of human conduct in a department of life too often dominated by force and fraud. It cannot be denied that the men who did this frequently confused the ideal with the real, and failed to distinguish with sufficient clearness between what ought to be and what is. But they rendered a great service to humanity when they obtained for their new science of International Law a place among the institutions the world was bound to recognise and develop.

The development of the science was the work of later writers, most of whom were men of affairs, experienced in the practical business of government and diplomacy, or advocates and judges in courts of law. They devoted their attention mainly to an investigation of the actual practices of states in their mutual dealings. From a study of negotiations, treaties and wars, they endeavoured to discover the rules by which states guided their conduct in the various exigencies of international life. But they connected themselves with the theories they inherited from their predecessors through the doctrine that the Law of Nature was what right reason dictated to mankind, and nothing contrary to it could be allowed. Having thus made their bow to the popular notion of Natural Law, they passed it by respectfully, and went on to build the edifice of their constructive work on the alternative Grotian foundation of general consent. Foremost among them were Bynkershoek, the Dutchman, and Vattel, the German-Swiss. The former was a lawyer by profession, and became President of the Supreme Court of Holland. In his *De Dominio Maris* and his *Quæstiones Juris Publici,* published in 1721 and 1737 respectively, he exalts custom as a source of the Law of Nations, and turns to treaties and the actions of statesmen and rulers as the best evidence of it. It is true he asserts that no human authority can prevail over right reason, but goes on to declare that in many cases reason may be doubtful, and then custom alone must decide. Moreover he shows no slavish deference to classical antiquity; for when he endeavours to deduce a rule of action from practice, we find that he takes his instances from recent history.

Vattel, whose *Droits des Gens* first saw the light in 1758, follows much the same method. He had held a diplomatic post under the Elector of Saxony, and was afterwards a Privy Councillor. In his great work he drew largely on the experience he had thus acquired. These two remarkable men, and others whom they influenced, worked mainly on positive lines, though they did not emancipate themselves entirely from the old naturalistic theories.

We must now turn to what I have called the Succession of Great Publicists. By this phrase I mean the series of writers on International Law who came too late to be reckoned among its founders, but whose works are nevertheless referred to as authoritative wherever in the civilised world men of competent knowledge discuss questions concerned with the mutual relations of states in peace or war. Their opinions are not, of course, held to be decisive. They are not lawgivers; they are only commentators on law. Their position in the chancelleries of the nations is somewhat analogous to that of Selden or Blackstone in an English Court. Just as a statement in the works of one of them could not override the plain sentences of a Statute passed by Parliament, so the printed word of a Wheaton, a Bluntschli, a Hall, a Von Martens or a Rivier could not prevail against an unequivocal clause of a great international treaty. But when a new point or a doubtful point is in dispute, the side which can quote such writers in its favour has a great advantage in argument over the side which can marshal to support it no views of world-renowned authorities. They are experts; and though all the world knows that experts may err, it is only the blatant and foolish portion of the world that pays no respect to expert opinion. Of course it often happens that such opinion is pretty evenly divided; and then all that can be done is to argue the matter out with the aid of the best materials and the best authorities that can be found. But the great writers on International Law do much more than discuss isolated theories or particular cases. They sift vast masses of matter,—piles of official documents, mountains of memoranda, stacks of treaties, libraries of history and biography—and reduce them to shape and order. They arrange and systematise. Out of their labours often comes a great improvement in some department of international intercourse that had hitherto been chaotic. Their subject owes to them whatever scientific form it may possess. The Apostolic Succession of jurists and publicists includes men of special knowledge in every quarter of the globe. The area from which writers on International Law are drawn has increased as fresh tracts have been won for civilisation and fresh peoples brought within the circle of the Family of Nations. The Western countries of Europe still hold their old pre-eminence; but its Eastern realms have entered into friendly competition with them, while the New World supplies a large contingent of recognised authorities drawn from both North and South America, and far away across illimitable tracts of ocean the political thinkers of Japan are producing works in French and English which are read with delight and quoted with respect wherever the *Jus Gentium* is studied and applied. The Law of Nations is as truly international in its expositors as it is in its provisions. From the beginning the authorities upon it were familiar with one another's writings and took note of one another's views. In spite of controversies and prejudices the greater among them exercised considerable influence over their fellows. By the beginning of the nineteenth century the various national rills that contributed their separate quotas towards the creation of the one great stream of true International Law had begun to combine together, and before it closed International Jurists had organised themselves into world-wide societies for meetings and discussions, and a noble river of justice and humanity was fertilising the wastes of diplomacy and war.

Side by side with the work of great writers we must consider the corresponding work of great Judges. When Grotius wrote, the sea-borne commerce of the modern world was in its infancy. It arose when the universal piracy which characterised the dark ages began to succumb to the efforts of enlightened rulers, the spread of improved views of morality, and the sense that more wealth was to be made by honest trade than by indiscriminate plunder. As soon as oceanic interchange of commodities became at all common, the goods of an enemy found at sea were regarded as the lawful prey of any belligerent who could send armed vessels to capture them. At once such questions as the following arose:—What were enemy's goods? Did their fate in any way depend on the national character of the ships that carried them? Could the goods of non-belligerents be captured, and, if so, under what circumstances? Might a warship make an attack anywhere on the waters, or were certain portions of them to be regarded as free from the operations of war? These and many other problems had to be settled by belligerent governments in the interests of their own internal law and order; for the proprietary rights of many of their citizens often depended upon them. Hence came the establishment of what we English call Courts of Admiralty in the maritime states of the Middle Ages, and the gradual growth of such mediæval Maritime and Commercial Codes as the Laws of *Oléron* and the more famous *Consolato del Mare.* But it was not till the modern epoch dawned at the time of the Reformation and the Renaissance that over-seas commerce took great strides forward. It was only beginning to do so in the middle of the seventeenth century, and consequently there is comparatively little to be found about it in the earliest treatises on International Law. But soon the questions just indicated, and many others also which were largely concerned with the rights and claims of neutrals, forced themselves into prominence. Then came the opportunity of the Courts of Admiralty and their judges. In England it was seized by Dr. Zouch and Sir Leoline Jenkins in the seventeenth century, and by the great Sir William Scott, afterwards Lord Stowell, at the end of the eighteenth and the beginning of the nineteenth. And during the same period in the young Republic of the United States Chief Justice Marshall made the most of a similar opening. As always happens, these great Judges really legislated. They stated the law, and in stating developed and improved it, while purporting to do no more than apply what already existed. Few abler judges than Lord Stowell have ever adorned the Bench, and to few has it been given to create to so great an extent that which he was in appearance merely administering. The law of maritime capture in time of war, prize-law as it is called, was a formless chaos when he went to the Court of Admiralty in 1798, and a reasoned system when he left it in 1828. The decisions of a Court of one nation in matters of international right as between belligerents, or belligerents and neutrals, are not of course legally binding on the Courts of another; but they are often quoted with a respect proportionate to the reputation of the Judge for learning and impartiality. In Lord Stowell's time foreign jurists, with the exception perhaps of those of the United States, were inclined to regard his decisions as biassed unduly by the belligerent interests of Great Britain. But after his death his work gradually permeated the whole body of accepted Prize Law, and many of the principles he laid down have been embodied in the Law of Nations through the operation of some of those Law-making Treaties which we must now briefly mention.

Hitherto in dealing with the growth of International

Law we have spoken of the consent of Nations as necessary to give it validity. But that consent has always meant tacit consent, a consent evidenced by common practice and the expressions of opinion to be found in the writings and declarations of prominent men in all the countries of the civilised world. Tacit consent is a plant of slow growth. It takes many years for a new opinion to march round the globe, or for a new rule to establish itself in the practice of all or most states. But in the infancy of the Society of Nations no one ever dreamed that its members could come together for the purpose of establishing by discussion and agreement rules of war, or even rules of peaceful intercourse. The utmost that could be done by way of common action was to gather together those who were belligerents in a great war, in order that by common conference they might settle the conditions of peace. This was accomplished successfully at the end of the terrible Thirty Years' War by the twin Congresses of Osnaburg and Münster in 1644-1648. But after an interval of nearly two centuries states began to make by treaties or other international instruments express agreements on points of International Law and practice. By the joint action of the Congresses of Vienna of 1815 and Aix-la-Chapelle of 1818 the rank and precedence of diplomatic ministers were settled, and in 1856 by a Declaration signed and negotiated at Paris along with the great Treaty which concluded the Crimean War the signatory powers in effect settled several disputed matters connected with the laws of war at sea.

This was a piece of informal international legislation, and since then the method of express consent has advanced by giant strides. In the next lecture we shall endeavour to trace its development; and meanwhile it will not be amiss to place on record the important fact that the great majority of those who have thought most seriously upon the international settlement that must come when the present war is over are convinced that the only firm basis on which a new international order can be established is common agreement embodied in great law-making treaties, and supported by sufficient force to compel obedience in the last resort.

LECTURE III.

INTERNATIONAL LAW AS IT STOOD IN JULY, 1914.

We have found in the course of our enquiries into the origin of modern International Law that from the beginning its rules were based to some extent on custom evidenced by general consent. But we have also seen that the consent referred to was tacit consent alone. It had to be deduced by a process of reasoning from the records of negotiations and wars, and the opinions of writers and speakers. Grotius declares that he made use of the testimony of philosophers, historians, poets and orators as witnesses to this consent. But nowhere does he cite any stipulation signed by all or most nations. And the reason is all-sufficient. In his time no such stipulations existed. Treaties there were in abundance; but none of them set forth rules of international conduct based on express agreement between those who came under them. Those assemblies of the representatives of many states which we call Congresses or Conferences were unknown. The first in European history were the Congresses of Osnaburg and Münster, which were really two divisions of one great gathering, the Protestant powers meeting at the first-named place, the Roman Catholic at the second.

But they assembled for the purpose of making peace after a great war, and not for the elaboration of general rules; and the same is true of their immediate successors. The two Congresses just mentioned gave us in 1648 the epoch-making Peace of Westphalia. The Congress of Ryswick arranged terms in 1697 between Louis XIV of France and his ally Spain on the one hand, and on the other the great coalition against him organised by William III of England. The Congress of Utrecht in 1713 ended formally the long struggle called in history the War of the Spanish Succession, though in effect the chief terms were arranged behind its back by the British and French Ministers. Neither of these, and none of those that followed during the eighteenth century, did more than lay down the conditions on which a group of warring powers were content to sheathe the sword. This alone was a great achievement. But it cannot be described as a step towards the evolution of anything even remotely resembling a legislature for states. The utmost we can say is that it created a position of honour and dignity for the big assemblies of authoritative and official national representatives which we call Conferences and our forefathers called Congresses. We must however note that these organs were very imperfectly developed. There was no general understanding as to what number of states must come together in order to constitute a Congress. Nor was there any rule as to the calling of Congresses. They happened more or less by accident, generally after a great war had been for some time in progress. Questions of honour and precedence at them occupied a most disproportionate amount of attention and energy. The shape of a table, for instance, was of great importance. As no agreement could be reached about the order of sitting at an ordinary long rectangular piece of furniture, round tables were introduced, and for a time all was harmony. Then some genius discovered that the place of honour at them was opposite the door, and chaos reigned again.[1] Now a better spirit exists, and these and similar matters are quietly settled by more or less formal agreement.

The first Congresses, then, were not general meetings of the Society of Nations and assumed no functions resembling in any way those of legislation. But a change began at Vienna in 1815. The assembled plenipotentiaries, who had come together to re-draw the map of Europe after the Napoleonic Wars, added to their labours by attacking certain other questions, especially those concerned with the use of great arterial rivers which are navigable from the sea for a long distance inland and run through the territory of two or more states. It is obvious that as soon as any of them becomes a highway of commerce many questions must arise as to the navigation of its waters. The primitive practice was to stretch an obstruction across the stream or erect a battery on its banks, and exact as heavy a toll as possible for permission to pass. For generations International Law took no notice of the matter. The questions which arose in connection with it were fought

[1] Lawrence, *International Problems and Hague Conferences*, p. 27.

out between the individuals or governments directly concerned. The results were so unsatisfactory that some form of international regulation was desired, and this the Congress of Vienna endeavoured to supply. It therefore added to its chief purpose of negotiating an European peace the further function of laying down general principles for dealing with these matters, and also with the Slave Trade, the rank of Diplomatic Representatives, and the neutralisation of Switzerland, all of which were held at length to be ripe for settlement by common consent. And on this occasion the consent was embodied in the formal words of a great international agreement, not inferred with much doubt and some hesitation from the more or less general practice of states. Mankind was approaching an epoch of something not altogether unlike legislation by express consent.

This method was applied to the creation of a new class of diplomatic agents in 1818, and the neutralisation of Belgium in 1831. But the next step forwards was taken in 1856, when the Conference which met in Paris to end the Crimean War not only embodied in the Treaty it drew up ways and means for the application to the Danube of the principle of freedom of navigation laid down in 1815, but also determined a number of disputed questions connected with the operations of maritime warfare. This last was done by a separate document negotiated at the same time as the Treaty, but not set forth in the clauses thereof. It was called the Declaration of Paris, to distinguish it from the

Treaty of Paris. The mere recitation of its provisions shews their great importance. They ran thus:

1. Privateering is and remains abolished.
2. The neutral flag covers enemy's goods with the exception of contraband of war.
3. Neutral goods with the exception of contraband of war are not liable to capture under the enemy's flag.
4. Blockades to be binding must be effective.

It was felt that such comprehensive developments of International Law required in order to give them assured validity the express consent of all, or at least the great majority, of the civilised states of the world. But seven powers only had gathered by their representatives round the Council-board in Paris. Accordingly it was agreed that the Declaration should be brought to the notice of those which had taken no part in the Congress, and that their formal accession should be invited. This proviso was accompanied by another to the effect that " the present Declaration is not, and shall not be, binding except between those powers who have acceded or shall accede to it." Within a few years the accession of nearly every state had been given, while the few who still held aloof acted in practice as if they had signed. Thus the principle of altering or adding to the Law of Nations by formal assent, which had been implied rather than stated by the Congress of Vienna in 1815, received direct endorsement in 1856 by the Congress of Paris. It did not of course diminish the validity of the tacit consent evidenced by general custom. But it introduced a new epoch of legislative or quasi-legislative activity.

At first it was a case of legislation without a legislature. No organised body existed whose function it was to make laws. There was only a general feeling that if all, or almost all, civilised states agreed together as to a rule of international intercourse, and signed a document to that effect, the rule in question was binding on the entire Society of Nations. But no one had authority to call states together for the consideration of such a rule. Advantage was taken, as we have just seen, of the assemblage of a great Congress or Conference for another purpose to get its members to make a few laws as a sort of by-product. These laws were in the beginning smuggled as it were into the Society of Nations as part of a Treaty of Peace. Then they were enshrined by themselves in a separate document, and the attention of the civilised world was pointedly called to it. The civilised world responded by acclaiming the new rules, and admitting them into the code which regulated the common life. Still it had not got beyond the point of regarding express consent as a valuable source of law. No procedure had been evolved for convening an assembly of states in order to take their opinion on proposals placed before them for discussion, nor was there any accepted method for formulating such proposals. Everything was left to the hazard of the moment, and any state that chose might take the initiative on the chance of being followed by the rest. Indeed it might come from private individuals in the first place, if only they could in the end induce some government to make corresponding diplomatic approaches to other governments.

This was the case with the first Geneva Convention, that of 1864. Two Swiss citizens, MM. Moynier and Dunant, witnessed the awful sufferings of the wounded at the battles of Magenta and Solferino in 1859, and were so horrified thereby that one of them wrote a terribly descriptive book on the subject, and both moved the Swiss Government to summon a Conference for the purpose of finding means to alleviate the miseries of the stricken soldiers. Twelve powers came together and adopted the principle of what was called the neutralisation of the sick and wounded, and also of all the persons and things concerned with the proper care of them. This principle was worked out in a great international document by the representatives of the twelve states who attended the Conference. The product of their labours was called the Geneva Convention from the place where it was drawn up. In the years that followed all other civilised powers signified their adhesion to it; and when in 1906 the time for revision came, the representatives of no less than thirty-six states attended a second Geneva Conference, and drew up a second Geneva Convention more complete and satisfactory than the first.

From the point of view of humanity the Geneva Convention of 1864 marked a great advance; but as regards the evolution of a legislative authority for states it registered no progress. It did but continue the method first adopted in 1856, when, as we have just seen, a comparatively few powers met and originated a great reform, but did not deem it binding except as between those who had originally adopted it, or had afterwards given their adhesion to it. The same thing may be said of the Declaration of St. Petersburg, negotiated in 1868 by the military delegates of eighteen states, who met together at the instance of the Emperor Alexander II of Russia, and endeavoured to place restrictions on the use of explosive bullets in war. They agreed to prohibit any projectile below 14 oz. in weight "which is either explosive or charged with fulminating or inflammable substances." But they did not deem their mission accomplished till all other civilised states had been invited to accede to the Declaration they had drawn up, and most had responded favourably. The case helps to show that in the middle of the last century states accepted, almost without knowing it, the principle that consent given in express words by all or most of the civilised powers of the world would turn a rule so supported into binding International Law, even when it was not deduced from general usage, but admittedly initiated a practice unknown before.

Moreover there seems to have been a feeling abroad that Europe must take the lead in these matters. None but European states were summoned to the Conference at Geneva in 1864, and of the eighteen who came together at St. Petersburg in 1868 only one, Persia, summoned because she had a permanent diplomatic representative at the Russian Court, was entirely non-European, a second, Turkey, being partly within and partly without the geographical limits of Europe. And further, when in 1874 Russian initiative again gathered together a Conference, this time at Brussels, for the purpose of elaborating an International Code for the conduct of war on land, none but European powers, if we may count Turkey as such, took part in the proceedings. On the other hand a little further on we find the United States of America represented, mainly for humanitarian reasons, in the Congo Conference of 1884 and the Brussels Anti-Slavery Conference of 1890.

This brings us to the first of the so-called Peace Conferences at The Hague. The date of it was 1899. At the end of an old century it sought to inaugurate a new era in international relations, and met with a far greater measure of success than is commonly supposed. If it failed in its first purpose, which was "the maintenance of the general peace, and a possible reduction of the excessive armaments which were burdening all nations," it nevertheless revealed to the world the possibility of creating an international legislature, and gave an enormous accession of strength to the cause of international arbitration. It may be doubted whether these things were contemplated by the original promoter of the Conference, Nicholas II, the weak and unfortunate Tsar whose career as a ruler has lately come to such an ignominious end. He has fallen now, and there are none so poor as to do him reverence; but when all that can be said against him has been uttered, it should be remembered in his favour that almost as soon as he entered the ranks of the world's high rulers he strove to use his new power to give effect to the idealism of his early youth.

Many things happened in the interval between 1874 and 1899. The world grew bigger in one sense and smaller in another—bigger, in that state after state in the New World and in Asia endeavoured as it became stronger and more civilised to play its part in the charmed circle of the Society of Nations, smaller, in that the old isolations were found to be no longer possible with the advent of quicker means of communication. This double process enlarged to a remarkable degree the horizon of statesmen. They had to take into consideration the views of governments and peoples who had been previously ignored. If Europe was still the centre it no longer contained the circumference also of the international circle. Though the old phrases about European civilisation, European public law and the European family of nations were constantly repeated, and for the matter of that are repeated still, virtue had begun to go out of them. It was felt that international society was as wide as the globe, and that the Great Powers were World Powers instead of merely European Powers. In consequence when Russia began to ventilate her new Tsar's ideas about peace and disarmament, her Foreign Office addressed a circular letter in 1898 to all the states who sent diplomatic representatives to the Court of St. Petersburg, whether they were European, American or Asiatic. Accordingly the representatives of twenty-six states assembled in 1899 in the Knights' Hall at The Hague. But this was only a beginning. When eight years afterwards the second Peace Conference came together, the widening process begun in 1899 was extended almost to the furthest limits possible. On the most liberal computation there are barely fifty civilised and independent states in the world. At The Hague in 1907 forty-four of them were represented, and of these twenty-one were European, nineteen American, and four Asiatic.

Before we pass on to consider the work of these Hague Conferences we must dwell for a few moments on their form. The first of them was a tentative effort to bring civilised mankind together by the representatives of their governments; and while it made a good beginning it did not achieve complete success in this respect. The second approached the end in view so very nearly that it may be held for all practical purposes to have attained it. The civilised world came together for the first time in history, and remained in consultation for four long months. This was in itself a wonderful achievement. It convinced the most sceptical of the reality of what many had regarded as a mere humanitarian dream; for no one can deny the existence of a Society of Nations when the records of a prolonged General Meeting can be produced to confute him. Nor is the significance of this great fact seriously diminished when it is pointed out, with a good deal of malice as well as a good deal of truth, that the procedure was chaotic, the results disproportionate to the labour expended, and the lofty professions of the leading states often belied by self-seeking and intrigue. It is a common device of the opponents of progress to decry the efforts of reformers on the ground that their work is not perfect nor their characters flawless. The existing order may have a thousand defects, and it is nevertheless supported. But if ten can be found in what is proposed as a substitute, the world rings with denunciation. The real question is not whether the new is perfect, but whether it is not so superior to the old as to make worth while, and more than worth while, the labour and upheaval of the change. And surely few will be found to declare that haphazard gatherings got together on the spur of the moment are better instruments of progress in the international sphere than solemn assemblies of all the powers whose voices have any reasonable title to be heard.

The second Hague Conference did undoubtedly contemplate a series of such gatherings, for in its Final Act it recommended "the assembly of a third Peace Conference, which might be held within a period corresponding to that which has elapsed since the preceding Conference, at a date to be fixed by common agreement between the Powers." The troubles in the Balkan peninsula, and the outbreak of the present war, prevented the carrying out of this recommendation, though a considerable amount of preparation for a third meeting had taken place. One of the great questions to be decided at the return of peace is whether the present rudimentary organisation is to be improved, or whether the powers are to lapse into the worse than barbaric condition of never coming together to deal with common affairs by common deliberations.

We can now see plainly that when the World-War broke out in 1914 the Society of Nations had been for almost exactly a century working its way towards an international legislature, and had almost reached the goal. Though the development was unconscious it was none the less real. It began by the recognition of express consent as a source of the laws which regulate the intercourse of states, side by side with the tacit consent embodied in binding customs. Then an organ was slowly evolved for the formal annunciation and registration of that express consent. This organ was a periodical assemblage of representatives of the governments of all civilised states. When in 1907 it came into action for the second time, its membership was well-nigh complete; but it found itself hampered at every turn by the absence of authoritative rules of procedure. Each state had a vote; yet in a rough and ready way votes were weighed as well as counted; and it was recognised that nothing was to be regarded as passed which was strongly opposed by a minority considerable either in numbers or in weight. The Conference was divided into Committees, but their work sometimes overlapped, and it depended on the will of a Chairman whether a given subject was discussed or ruled out as irrelevant. The question of giving votes on a basis of population, wealth, or territory, or some combination of all these, was too thorny to be discussed. But the further question of preparing the business beforehand, and bringing out a programme which the Governments concerned could study in advance, was carefully considered, with the result that a very reasonable proposition was put forward in the Final Act of the Conference of 1907. It was suggested that "some two years before the probable date of the meeting (of a third Conference) a preparatory Committee should be charged by Governments with the task of collecting the various proposals to be submitted to the Conference, of ascertaining what subjects are ripe for embodiment in an International Regulation, and of preparing a programme which the Governments should decide upon in sufficient time to enable it to be carefully examined by the countries interested." It added that "This committee should further be entrusted with the task of proposing a system of organisation and procedure for the Conference itself."

An agitation for the appointment of this International Committee was going on, and some states had already set small groups of officials and experts to work in gathering information and forming conclusions for their own guidance, when the great catastrophe of the World-War overwhelmed us. Then came the day when the firm foundations of the earth rocked beneath our feet, and the light of the sun of progress was quenched in the red mist of war. Before we attempt to describe the overthrow let us look round, and see how the fabric of International Law stood on the fateful 31st July, 1914.

We find in the first place the beginnings of an Arbitral Jurisprudence. The reference to Arbitration of disputes between states which the parties concerned are not able to settle for themselves is almost as old as war. Instances of it can be found in Greek History, and indeed in nearly all history if we give a wide interpretation to the phrase. The *Vir pietate gravis*, the man weighty because of his character, has been called in by savage tribes, as well as by cultured Hellenic cities, to compose their quarrels, and prevent by a just decision an appeal to the sword. But Arbitration as an organised system for referring to acknowledged experts in the laws and customs of states differences between two or more of them which their diplomacy cannot clear up, is a product of the nineteenth century. It presupposes two things neither of which had a vigorous and widespread existence till then. The first is a system of legal rules and accepted customs covering many, if not all, of the occasions likely to arise in the mutual intercourse of states; and the second is a considerable body of men well versed in these laws and customs, and able by reason of their ability and integrity to apply them without fear or favour to the cases brought under their notice. All through the century International Law grew apace. Towards the end of it the conviction that in four cases out of five it was safe to arbitrate spread rapidly. After the important Geneva Arbitration of 1872 between Great Britain and the United States, on what were termed collectively the Alabama Claims, the cases became much more numerous, and took more decidedly the form of pleading between parties before a High Court of Justice. It is almost impossible to obtain figures that are absolutely correct, but we may say without much risk of contradiction that there were about 177 cases from 1794 to the end of 1900,[1] and add that between 1900 and 1917 as many as 50 more can be found. As a rule Arbitrators were chosen not because they were kings and rulers, or even men of high character and sound judgment who could be expected to reach an equitable decision by the light of nature, but because they had special knowledge of the *Jus Gentium,* and might be trusted to give judgment according to its rules and principles. States were far more willing to submit their claims to an expert in a known law than they had been to invoke the aid of a non-professional umpire. In that frame of mind they came to the first Hague Conference in 1899, and there agreed to provide the Society of Nations with what they called a Permanent Court of Arbitration. What follows shows that this was a misnomer; but the institution to which it was applied marked a very great advance in the provision of means for the Pacific Settlement of International Disputes. Every power which signed the Convention with this title negotiated at the Conference, received the right of nominating "four persons at the most, of known competency in questions

[1] Dr. James Brown Scott, *The Hague Conferences,* Vol. I, pp. 224-225.

of International Law, of the highest moral reputation, and disposed to accept the duties of Arbitrator." [1] From the long list thus obtained the powers which decide to have recourse to the so-called Permanent Court may choose their judges by agreement between themselves. But if they fail to agree, each side is to nominate two from the list, and these four together choose an Umpire. To this it was added in 1907 that only one of the two chosen by each party can be its citizen or an Arbitrator nominated by it. What is permanent in this arrangement is not the Court, but the list of persons from among whom the Court is to be constituted. There it is always; though the individuals of whom it is composed may change. Each is appointed for six years, and may be reappointed by his government at the end of that time.

But though strictly speaking there is no Permanent Court the continuous existence of the means of making a Court whenever it is wanted is a great improvement upon the previous state of affairs, when two disputants already heated by a diplomatic controversy had to agree at the last moment not only on the employment of an Arbitral Tribunal, but also on how to create it and what its procedure should be. These last matters are dealt with in the Hague Convention for the Pacific Settlement of International Disputes as negotiated in 1899 and revised in 1907.[2] But it must be

[1] See Article 23 of the Convention of 1899, and Article 44 of the similar Convention of 1907.

[2] See Chs. II-IV.

carefully noted that there is nothing compulsory about the whole scheme. The powers who made it did not thereby bind themselves to use the machinery they created. They need not arbitrate at all; or, if they arbitrate, they may call into existence a tribunal fashioned according to any plan that seems good to them at the time, or, if they use the Hague Tribunal, they may vary the prescribed procedure as they think fit.

The Peace Conference of 1907 went so far as to proclaim in its Final Act its unanimity "in admitting the principle of compulsory arbitration," but lamented its inability to conclude a General Convention in that sense. Nevertheless it gave a broad hint[1] to the powers to conclude among themselves particular Conventions binding the parties to arbitrate in all cases not specially excepted in the agreement itself; and this hint has been followed by the negotiation of nearly two hundred such Conventions. It also made a serious and long-sustained effort to create a great High Court of Arbitral Justice which, like the Law Courts of civilised states, should have a continuous existence and sit at regular intervals to deal with any disputes which might be brought before it. But the attempt failed owing to the insistence by some states on the application of the principle of equality to such matters as the appointment of Judges. In the end the Conference had to be content with calling the attention of the Signatory Powers to "the advisability of adopting thc annexed draft

[1] Hague Convention of 1907, *For the Pacific Settlement of International Disputes,* Art. 40.

Convention for the creation of a Judicial Arbitration Court, and of bringing it into force as soon as an agreement has been reached respecting the selection of the Judges and the constitution of the Court.[1]

After making all possible deductions on account of this and other failures, we cannot but come to the conclusion that by the end of the year 1907 a very great step had been taken towards the creation of a world-wide system of Arbitral Courts. Especially is this borne in upon us when we remember that fourteen international controversies have been settled by Hague Tribunals since they were called into existence in 1899. Some of these quarrels, like the age-long Atlantic Fisheries dispute between Great Britain and America, had more than once brought powerful states to the verge of war. Moreover many more differences that diplomacy failed to remove have yielded to the influence of boards of Arbitration created by the parties themselves. Of course International Law grew in the process of application. As the number of Arbitrations increased something like an Arbitral Jurisprudence began to spring up; and we know from experience of our own British and American legal procedure that the invocation of precedents often leads to an almost imperceptible extension of the rules on which they are based.

This mention of rules brings us to the further conclusion, that there was when the war broke out in the Summer of 1914 a rapidly increasing Statute Book of

[1] *Final Act of the Hague Conference of 1907*, Vœu 1.

the Law of Nations. To make the matter quite clear we must refer back for a moment to what has been already said regarding the general recognition of express consent as a source of International Law. Directly states were agreed on this their willingness to make new rules, or clear up disputed interpretations of old ones, would depend upon the strength or weakness of their sense of a need for them. We have seen that the general consciousness of such need was so great that the institution called the Hague Conference, originally devised as an expedient of the moment to fulfil another purpose, was when the World-War broke out in process of being turned into a permanent organ for the satisfaction of legislative necessities. The first of the two so-called Peace Conferences that have been held at The Hague produced three Conventions—one for the Pacific Settlement of International Disputes, one concerning the Laws and Customs of War on Land, and one for the Adaptation of the Principles of the Geneva Convention to Maritime Warfare. These Conventions were in effect International Statutes binding the signatory powers, and the same may be said of the Declarations embodied in the Final Act. The one Resolution which affirmed the desirability of the restriction of military budgets, but took no steps towards the attainment of this desirable end, cannot be placed in the same category; neither can the six Wishes which merely set forth a programme for the future. The second Conference succeeded in negotiating no less than thirteen Conventions. These of course are International Statutes in the same sense as the Conventions of the first Conference; and what has just been said of its Declarations, Resolutions and Wishes applies with equal force to those of the second. The two together have produced a large number of quasi-legislative documents, some of which rise in length and importance almost to the dimensions of codes. In addition we have to remember that even if we rule out of account the little bits of legislation sometimes contained in treaties dealing with other matters, there are pre-Hague documents, such as the Declarations of Paris and St. Petersburg and the two Geneva Conventions, that must rank along with the legislative transactions of the Conferences. Taking them together they form a considerable volume which we may with justice call the first Statute Book of the Law of Nations. And in giving it that exalted name, we may venture to hope that it will in time be followed by many similar volumes. But we must be on our guard against the assumption that this Statute Book contains all the rules which states are bound to observe in their mutual relations. Those based on tacit consent must be added. The two together make up the observances which have gained authority in the Society of Nations. It is impossible to go through the whole code or any considerable part of it in a single lecture; but special attention must be called to two or three matters, if we are to obtain a clear idea of how International Law stood in the early Summer of 1914. We will begin with the attempts which were made from time to time to codify the Laws of War on Land. Their history illustrates in a remarkable way the gradual growth of International Law, showing the influence of both custom and express consent, and containing excellent examples of the work of private individuals, Associations, and Governments.

A large share of the labours of Grotius was devoted, as we saw in the first lecture, to the improvement of the laws of war, and undoubtedly his writings had a great effect in humanising them. In spite of occasional lapses into savagery there was a steady improvement in them from his time to the Wars of the French Revolution, and again from 1815 onwards. But no attempt was made to bring them together in one comprehensive set of regulations till 1863, when in the midst of the American Civil War the Government of Washington issued "Instructions" for the guidance of its armies. These were compiled by Dr. Lieber, a learned German who had emigrated in his youth to the United States, and became an American citizen. His work was well done; and the example of President Lincoln in providing the Federal troops with such a guide was followed by the rulers of several important states. But no attempt was made to create a common Code for all states by international agreement till 1874, when at the instance of Alexander II of Russia a Conference of representatives of fourteen European powers was held at Brussels for the purpose of drawing up such a body of rules, based upon the best customs of the most enlightened nations and containing what improvements and modifications could command general assent. The Conference succeeded in performing the task of codification assigned to it. In the process it made much use of the American "Instructions." Its Code was by no means complete, but it embodied as far as it went a high standard of humanity and respect for the life, property and honour of non-combatant civilians. But for a variety of reasons its work failed to obtain ratification from the Governments concerned, and therefore had none of the binding force that comes from express consent. The matter was next taken up by the *Institut de Droit International,* an Association of the leading International Jurists of the civilised world, who meet together from time to time to discuss legal questions connected with the mutual relations of states. After long study and much debate they passed a Manual of the Laws of War on Land at their Oxford Session in 1880. It had, of course, no binding force on nations and governments, but, like other pronouncements of the *Institut,* it possesses the authority which the considered opinion of the best experts in a given subject must always have with intelligent people. It, and the Brussels Declaration, and the American "Instructions" were the chief sources of the famous *Règlement* attached to the Hague "Convention concerning the Laws and Customs of War on Land." This was drawn up at the first Peace Conference in 1899, and revised at the Second in 1907. The Convention to which it was appended did not include the Regulations themselves. But it bound the signatory powers to issue to their armed land forces instructions in conformity with them;[1] and by stipulating that the provisions contained in them "are only binding between the contracting powers, and only if all the belligerents are parties to the Convention,"[2] it certainly implied that in all other circumstances they were binding. Moreover the revised Convention of 1907 contained a new Article, which declares that a belligerent which violated the Convention should be liable to make compensation, and should be responsible for all acts committed by persons forming part of its armed forces.[3] In the face of stipulations like these it is idle to argue, as Germany does, that nothing beyond a sort of platonic approval of the Code is required from the powers who accepted the Convention.[4]

The Code or *Règlement* is by no means complete. Certain matters were deliberately omitted, such as reprisals, and the treatment of those who are sometimes called war-rebels, because, as the preamble to the Convention says, it is not possible "to agree forthwith on provisions embracing all the circumstances that may occur in practice." But that same preamble went on to guard especially against the assumption "that the cases not provided for should, for want of a written provision, be left to the arbitrary judgment of the military commanders." It did so in the remarkable

[1] *Hague Convention concerning the Laws and Customs of War on Land,* Art. 1.

[2] *Ibid.,* Art. 2.

[3] *Ibid.,* Art. 3. (1907.)

[4] See Introduction to *Kriegsbrauch im Landkriege* (The German Official War Book).

words that "Until a more complete Code of the laws of war can be issued, the High Contracting Parties think it expedient to declare that in cases not included in the Regulations adopted by them, populations and belligerents remain under the protection and the rule of the principles of the law of nations, as they result from the usages established between civilised peoples, from the laws of humanity, and the requirements of the public conscience." It is curious to reflect that the signature of a German plenipotentiary was affixed to this document only eleven years ago, and still more curious to attempt to fathom "the requirements of the public conscience" of Germany. Apparently this peculiar faculty condemns common courtesy and humanity to prisoners of war, approves of the destruction of sick and wounded who believe themselves in safety under the Red Cross, and applauds the drowning at sea of helpless women and children.

The next point to be emphasised is that by the middle of the year 1914 parts of the Law of War at Sea had been settled, while the unratified Declaration of London of 1909 and the unofficial Oxford *Manuel* of 1913 represented attempts to settle other portions also. Among the subjects dealt with by the Second Peace Conference at The Hague were submarine mines, bombardments by naval forces, the duties and immunities of hospital ships, the exemption from capture of coast fishing boats and certain other craft, the legal position of enemy merchant vessels at the outbreak of hostilities, the conversion of merchantmen into warships, and the rights and duties of neutral states in maritime warfare. On this great cluster of subjects authoritative rules were laid down, sometimes in a thorough and satisfactory manner, sometimes very incompletely. Taken as a whole they marked a great advance towards a real code for the regulation of war at sea. Moreover the process commenced by the Hague Conference of 1907 was carried on by the much smaller Naval Conference of London summoned by Great Britain in the autumn of 1908. Early in 1909 it produced the ill-starred Declaration of London, whose misfortune was that it came either too late or too soon—too late for the regulation of a sea-order about to perish owing to advances of science and retrogressions of morality, and too soon for the regulation of a new order whose outlines are yet in the making. It failed as we all know; but had it succeeded it would have given the authority of the leading maritime states to a great act of reconciliation and construction. A similar statement cannot of course be made concerning the *Manuel* of the laws of war as between belligerents passed at the Oxford meeting of the Institute of International Law in 1913. But we may say of it that it shewed statesmen with what clearness and impartiality jurists can handle the legal intricacies that arise from a great conflict at sea.

The third and final matter to be noted in connection with the period of quasi-legislative activity we have been considering is that within it the Judicial Arbitration Court previously mentioned and also an International Prize Court of Appeal were planned and well-nigh established. The Declaration of London would have settled, had the old order continued, age-long differences between the powers with regard to Blockade, Contraband of War, Unneutral Service, and various minor matters. Could this have been done two most important consequences would have followed. On the one hand the way would have been paved for the advent of a complete Code for the regulation of war at sea, and its adoption by the express consent of all maritime states, and on the other hand the last obstacles would have been removed from the path of the International Prize Court of Appeal which the powers decided in 1907 to set up, according to a wise and statesmanlike plan embodied in the Twelfth Convention of the Second Hague Conference. But the failure of the Declaration of London to secure ratification sealed the fate of the International Prize Court. No one wanted a Court of Final Appeal, when the law it was to administer remained uncertain as to matters of the utmost importance. If such a Court comes at all, it will come as a part of the new and better system for the regulation of maritime conflicts which must be established after the war, if sea-borne commerce is to continue and neutrals to be preserved from outrage and ruin. A blessed reaction from the brutality of to-day may give the next generation its Judicial Arbitration Court, and its International Prize Court of Appeal also.

We may sum up by saying that when the fateful moment came in the Summer of 1914 there was a real and world-wide Society of Nations so far organised as to possess a Quasi-legislative Assembly, a rapidly growing system of law, a rudimentary judiciary, and a small executive, which last is to be found in the International Bureau and the Permanent Administrative Council at The Hague.[1] Till a few weeks before the storm broke there was a reasonable prospect of the rapid growth of this Society. It seemed to be developing special organs for the performance of functions essential to the welfare of all its members, without destroying the national independence and State Sovereignty of each. The extension and improvement of its laws, the strengthening of its tribunals, and the bringing into existence of efficient means for the restraint of unruly powers, appeared to have come within the limits of possibility. The more sanguine among us deemed that they might in a few decades be the prizes of wise and sustained effort. But we have witnessed retrogression instead of progress; and we can see now that the order we hoped to mould to our ideals contained within itself germs of destruction. It lacked any means of obliging its members to bestir themselves for the enforcement of the performance of their common duties. Each state was bound to obey the rules of the International Society; but no state was bound, in the absence of express stipulations, to see that other states obeyed them. The result was that any ill-disposed member might violate its obligations, not exactly with impunity, but with nothing certain in the way of penalty or compulsion. Others might

[1] *Hague Convention for the Pacific Settlement of International Disputes,* Ch. II.

interfere, or again they might not. There was a chance of castigation, but a chance of impunity also. Further we have discovered by awful experience that science can be the handmaid of destruction with quicker efficiency than she can be the builder of comfort and happiness. War has now invaded the air above and the depths below. And what we experience to-day is but a beginning. It seems as if no limit can be set to the possibilities of slaughter and ruin which lurk in the development of modern armaments. Moreover the organisation of nations for war has made such rapid strides that the old distinction between combatants and non-combatants is on the point of vanishing altogether. And lastly the German doctrine of *Kriegsraison,* which is in brief that any accepted restraint in warfare may be set aside to gain a useful advantage or save a severe disaster,[1] has ceased to be the vagary of a few professors and become the creed of the greatest military power in the world. What all this has meant I shall attempt to describe in the next lecture.

[1] Holtzendorff, *Handbuch des Völkerrechts,* Vol. IV, §§ 65, 66.

LECTURE IV.

THE PARTIAL OVERTHROW OF INTERNATIONAL LAW.

Not long ago I was sitting at breakfast opposite to a young and thoughtful medical man who had spent a year in service at the front. Our hostess passed him a copy of the syllabus of these lectures, and asked his opinion on it. He answered by a criticism on the present title—The Partial Overthrow of International Law. "I should call the overthrow complete," said he. My answer was, "That is just what I expected you to say. But I am sure you are wrong. A very large part of International Law is concerned with the pacific intercourse of states, and that part remains almost untouched. It is the rules that deal with war and neutrality which have been broken into fragments."

This seems to me to sum up the situation accurately. The outlook is indeed bad, so bad that I doubt whether we can find its like since the Thirty Years' War came to an end in 1648. But we need not make it out to be worse than it is. Much of the fabric of the *Jus Gentium* stands intact, and much more is capable of repair. But before we can profitably discuss the question of rebuilding, we must survey the ruins carefully and endeavour to decide where it is necessary to lay fresh foundations, where we can make use of foundations already in existence, and where we may rest content with a few judicious repairs to walls and towers. To execute this survey is the object of the present lecture, and to discuss the most effective methods of rebuilding will be the task of the two that follow.

It will be wise to begin our examination by recalling what was said at the end of the last lecture about the absence of any general obligation to enforce existing laws. As we have seen, they rest upon express or tacit consent; and the kind of consent given or understood on the part of a state is a consent to observe them in its own conduct. No promise is made to act the part of policeman, and enforce them on others who ought to obey them, but do not. An obligation of this latter kind is assumed only in the case of Treaties of Guarantee, and they are rare. In the early stages of the present war, when the calculated atrocities of the German troops in Belgium were horrifying the civilised world, the United States were sometimes blamed in England because they took no steps to secure the observance by Germany of the Hague Convention of 1907 on the Rights and Duties of Neutral Powers and Persons in War on Land, though they were among the signatory powers. Those who put forward this view can hardly have read the Convention. If they had, they would have found no stipulation binding the parties to prevent or punish one another's violations. Instead there is in Article 5 a provision to the effect that a neutral power "is not bound to punish acts in violation of neutrality unless such acts have been committed on its own territory." America, as an independent state, had the right to make war or remain at peace as she thought fit. At first she chose to remain outside the conflict; but at length there came a time when the outrageous treatment of her Government and her citizens by Germany forced her to enter it; and when she did so her determination was sharpened by indignation at German breaches of neutral rights all over the world. But the fact that she had signed Conventions which Germany constantly violated imposed on her no legal obligation to take up arms in order that the offending state might be forced to keep its plighted word.

When a Treaty of Guarantee is in question the case is different. The parties to such a treaty bind themselves not only to observe it in their own proper persons, but also to prevent the violation of it by others. For instance when the Kingdom of Belgium was established by the Great Powers of Europe early in the last century, they guaranteed its independence and perpetual neutrality by the treaties of 1831 and 1839. They thus bound themselves to interfere on its behalf should it be attacked, as long as it observed the condition of abstaining from any warlike or diplomatic action that had other ends in view than the protection of its integrity and neutrality. We must remember that in the thirties of last century the Great Powers of Europe were five in number, the five being Great Britain, France, Austria, Prussia, and Russia. In the place of Prussia now stands the German Empire, which in the affairs of the Society of Nations has assumed the legal clothing of the old Prussian Kingdom. In 1870 when it was in the intermediate stage of development from the one to the other, and was called the North German Confederation, it not only acknowledged that it inherited the obligation to respect the Belgian frontiers in its war with France, but held up the latter power to the reprobation of the civilised world because of a secret intrigue against Belgian independence in which Napoleon III, when Emperor, had been skilfully entangled by Bismarck. Since then Germany has on several occasions admitted its obligations towards its weak but prosperous neighbour, and proclaimed its resolution to observe them. As late as 1913, Herr Von Jagow, its Foreign Secretary, declared in the Budget Committee of the Reichstag that "Belgian Neutrality is determined by international Conventions which Germany is resolved to respect."

The statesmen of Belgium were nervously anxious to do nothing that would give an ambitious neighbour a pretext for charging them with a breach of neutral obligations. They did well to be careful. The position of their country between France and Germany made it open to invasion from either; and it had not sufficient strength to protect itself against a great military power, though it strained its resources in fortifying its frontiers and increasing its army. But there was always the reassuring consciousness that its "neutralisation," as it was called, was recognised as an essential part of the public law of Europe.[1]

As a matter of fact the little kingdom remained unmolested for the greater part of a century. When it was in danger during the Franco-Prussian War in 1870 Great Britain was ruled by one of the most pacific administrations that ever controlled her destinies. Nevertheless she stood boldly by the side of her weak neighbour, and covenanted to assist in the defence of its neutrality against whichever of the two belligerents might venture to attack it. The result was that neither made any hostile attempt; and for many years Belgium felt comparatively safe. France became its sincere friend, while British solicitude on its behalf was in no way abated.[2] But towards the close of the last century it became apparent that Germany in her restless search for points of vantage, and easy roads into France unbarred by fortresses and entrenched camps, was casting greedy eyes across the Belgian frontiers. German strategic railways, unwanted for any purposes of commerce, were built in close proximity to its borders, and a school of German publicists declared in no obscure terms that its territory ought to form part of the Fatherland. Still constant protestations of friendliness were made by the German Government, and any intention of violating Belgian neutrality was disclaimed. The last assurance was given on July 31, 1914, when

[1] Léon Van Der Essen, *The Invasion,* Ch. I.

[2] Ellery C. Stowell, *The Diplomacy of the War of 1914,* pp. 4-7.

Herr Von Below, the German Minister at Brussels, informed the Belgian Foreign Office that he was certain the views of his government had not changed. He repeated this statement on August 2nd, yet a few hours afterwards this same diplomatist demanded free passage through Belgium for the German Armies on pain of instant hostilities if it was refused! [1]

But this was not the worst. Scarcely was the treacherous deed consummated, and the shamefaced excuse of the German Chancellor made that its wrongfulness was justified by its overwhelming necessity, than all sorts of falsehoods were trumped up to shew that it was not a wrong at all, but a righteous retribution. There was the cock-and-bull story of the motor cars driven by disguised French officers through Belgian territory to attack the Rhineland,[2] the fictitious tales of British marines in Ostend and French guns in Liège some days before the commencement of hostilities, and the mendacious reports of French military violations of the German frontier which were deemed sufficient justification for the charge that France was about to march her forces through Belgium to the invasion of Germany.[3] Then, as time went on and the German troops were stained deeper and deeper every day with the crimes that accompanied their occupation

[1] Léon Van Der Essen, *The Invasion,* Chs. II and III.

[2] Proclamation issued by General Von Emmich on August 4, 1914, and given in Appendix C of the Report of the Bryce Committee on the Alleged German Outrages [Cd. 7895, p. 183].

[3] Ellery C. Stowell, *The Diplomacy of the War of 1914,* pp. 419-421.

of Belgian territory, while German statesmen were more closely entangled in the web of their own fictions and contradictions, a discovery was made by their agents in the archives at Brussels. It consisted of a few notes of discussions between Belgian and British officers in 1906 and 1912 with a view to concerting measures of defence should the necessity for them arise. These conversations were immediately described as Conventions, and published to the world with the deliberate perversion of an important passage. They were accompanied by a triumphant commentary to the effect that Belgium had by her own act and deed abandoned her neutrality long before the war, and was only reaping the just reward of breaking her treaty obligations and plotting against her Teutonic neighbour. No one can for a moment imagine that German statesmen are not well aware of the difference between planning a crime and planning the means of preventing a crime. But it suited them to ignore it; and ever since their obsequious press has been repeating the calumny they invented, and their tame jurists have been engaged in demonstrating that the treaties they falsely accuse Belgium of violating either never did protect Belgian territory, or have been cancelled by subsequent documents, or destroyed by change of circumstances. These and a number of other mutually contradictory propositions do but serve to shew that German hatred of those whom Germany has so shamelessly injured has deprived her authorities of all sense of logic in argument or decency in action.[1] They first ravished Belgium and then slandered her. For pure, sheer, unmitigated blackguardism their conduct can only be compared to that of some vile guardian who, having overcome by a mixture of force and fraud the resistance of a blameless ward, brazenly maintains, in order to shield himself from general reprobation, that she had previously been little better than a common woman. And let us not forget that the German outrage is continuous. It is not merely that one unlawful and cowardly blow has been struck, one foul crime committed. The armies of Germany still stand on the violated territory, the satraps of Germany still plunder and oppress the Belgian nation, and the German campaign of calumny against them still goes glibly on. There can be no safety for the Society of Nations, no vindication before the world of good faith and rudimentary justice, till, failing the repentance and complete reparation of which there are no signs, the perjured rulers are made to relinquish their prey, and the robber hosts are shattered in a mighty overthrow.[2]

At present we have but begun the indictment against the powers responsible for the ruin of some of the noblest parts of the great structure that goes by the name of International Law. It would be wrong to

[1] Professor Ch. de Visscher, *Belgium's Case,* Ch. III; Ellery C. Stowell, *The Diplomacy of the War of 1914,* pp. 376-456, 626-638. The documents given in these passages render superfluous further reference to the voluminous literature of the subject; but it may be well to add that an impartial summary of the points at issue concerning the military conversations will be found in Bevan, *The Method in the Madness,* pp. 205-212.

[2] It seems now (Nov., 1918) as if both these anticipations would soon be realised.

represent them as the only sinners in a Society where absolute integrity had hitherto been the rule. But this we may, nay must, say. They have done deliberately, systematically and continuously what others may have done in moments of passion, spasmodically and occasionally. Moreover they have done it so thoroughly that if their foul web of falsehood and deceit is not completely unravelled, and their offence severely punished, good faith will vanish from the future of international transactions, and civilised humanity will sink back into the condition of Italy in the time of Cæsar Borgia. And unfortunately what is true of faith and honour is true of justice and mercy also. They, too, are in danger. There is nothing so catching as successful crime. German "frightfulness" has inflicted a severe blow on that sense of the binding nature of mortal law which has often been a great restraining power in the midst of warfare and bloodshed. Unless the German nation and its rulers and satellites are taught by painful, but blessed, experience that their utter disregard of all the laws of humanity in war does not bring them one inch nearer their ultimate aims, but on the contrary arrays against them the greater part of the civilised world, there is little hope of the future of the human race. It cannot hug a cancer to its bosom, and expect to escape rottenness and destruction.

The accusation against Germany and her allies is not, let us remember, that their troops have sometimes got out of hand, and been guilty of abominable deeds. This happens occasionally in all armies, even the best disciplined. It stands to reason that every great host must contain a certain number of ruffians, and that every war must give to some of them greater opportunities for indulging their worst propensities than occur in civil life. Moreover it is a well-known fact that privation, or the excitement of furious conflict, or the sight of cruelly-injured comrades, will sometimes madden troops, and cause men who are ordinarily well-behaved to indulge in orgies of drunkenness, lust, and cruelty. Humane commanders strive their best to prevent these atrocities; and as the world has grown more civilised they have become rarer and rarer. But there is little prospect of stamping them out altogether. Only if all men were perfect could it be done; but then there would be no war. I am not thinking of things like these when I declare that German "frightfulness" is a danger to the whole fabric of human Society. What I have in my mind are the breaches of the laws of war deliberately planned by the German High Command, and systematically carried out by soldiers acting under orders in most cases, but in some perhaps only given to understand that if they robbed, or burnt, or violated, or slew, no notice would be taken of it.

Is there any sane man in the whole world who now believes that no atrocities were committed on the population when the German armies invaded Belgium? That, it will be remembered, was the first assertion that proceeded from the Fatherland in answer to the chorus of horror provoked by the deeds of its soldiers. The next was that the burnings and shootings complained of were a just punishment for cruel and foul outrages committed on German wounded and stragglers by Belgian civilians. We need not be so quixotic as to declare that no peasant could ever have shot or stabbed a soldier who had lost his way, or no woman ever mutilated a wounded enemy. But when we remember that the Government of Belgium took every possible means by proclamations and by seizure of arms to remove from the civil population both the will and the means of resistance, and when we read the flimsy stories of anonymous witnesses that the German official publications expect us to regard as evidence, we are more than sceptical of any rising against the invaders in any district, or of the commission upon them of any appreciable number of cruelties.[1] Instead, there is strong evidence for the belief that the general attitude of the peasantry was one of pitiable and hopeless terror. They made constant attempts to conciliate the German soldiery by gifts of food and drink and portable property.[2] On the other hand how is it possible to explain the appliances for fire-raising carried by the invading troops, the carefully-prepared means for the packing and removing of loot, the damning confessions found

[1] This is the main argument of the German White Book on the Alleged Offenses against International Law in the conduct of the war. It, and the evidence brought forward in support of it, are subjected to a most damaging analysis by Professor T. H. Morgan in the introductory chapter of his *German Atrocities.*

[2] The evidence of Mr. L. Mokveld, a Dutch journalist who was on the spot in the early days of August, 1914, is conclusive as to this. See his book, *The German Fury in Belgium,* pp. 68, 69, 77, 92-94, and other passages.

in private letters, and the ferocious threats of German proclamations,[1] except by a plan to terrorise the people of both hostile and neutral countries, and force them to believe that nothing but ruin could come from opposition to German demands? It is here that the abominable doctrine of *Kriegsraison* comes in. It holds that since there is a great military advantage in filling the breasts of enemies, actual or possible, with abject fear, therefore whatever does this is allowable, even though forbidden by the ordinary laws of war. For "it cannot be denied that in cases of real necessity ravage, burning and devastation, even on a large scale as of whole neighbourhoods and tracts of country, may be practised, where it is not a question of any particular determinate result of strategical operation, but only of more general measures, in order, for instance, to make the further advance of the enemy impossible, or even to shew him what war is in earnest when he persists in carrying it on without serious hope." [2]

The policy inaugurated during the first weeks of the war has been continued ever since. After a time the indiscriminate shootings, outrages and burnings in Belgium ceased. But we are not likely to forget Dinant, Aerschot and Louvain, though Brussels still stands, and Bruges has not been systematically looted, and the

[1] Overwhelming evidence on these points is to be found in the Appendix to the Bryce Report, and the Belgian and French Reports. Their specific allegations are not disproved by general denials, an aspect of the case admirably presented by Bevan, *The Method in the Madness*, pp. 215-225.

[2] Holtzendorff, *Handbuch des Völkerrechts*, Vol. IV, p. 484.

women of Ghent have hitherto escaped wholesale violation. But the wicked system of which the first atrocities were the product is still applied though in somewhat different forms. The Hague *Règlement,* or Code for War on Land, says, "Neither requisitions in kind nor services can be demanded from communes or inhabitants except for the necessities of the army of occupation. They must be in proportion to the resources of the country." [1] The Germans have stripped the country of supplies and left the bulk of the people to be fed by a charitable organisation in neutral hands, indulging now and then in the sport of torpedoing a grain ship carrying food for their victims under a safe-conduct granted by their own authorities.

The Hague *Règlement* prohibits the levy of money contributions above and beyond the ordinary taxes in the occupied territory, except "for military necessities or the administration of such territory." [2] The Germans have in countless instances exacted forced contributions to an enormous extent amounting by this time to something like seventy millions sterling. In addition they have taken machinery, goods and raw material, as well as cash and securities, and this in spite of the plain proviso, "Private property cannot be confiscated." [3] And be it remembered that all this takes no account of the requisitions levied in kind which were dealt with in the previous paragraph.

The Hague *Règlement* forbids a belligerent "to destroy or seize the enemy's property, unless such de-

[1] Article 52. [2] Article 49. [3] Article 46.

struction or seizure be imperatively demanded by the necessities of War," [1] and provides that " in sieges and bombardments all necessary steps should be taken to spare as far as possible buildings devoted to religion, art, science and charity, historic monuments, hospitals, and places where the sick and wounded are collected, provided that they are not used at the same time for military purposes." [2] The Germans have destroyed many of them, including some of the most beautiful examples in the world of mediæval architecture, such as the Library of Louvain and the Cloth Hall of Ypres.

The Hague *Règlement* lays down that services demanded by the invaders must not be " of such a nature as to imply for the population any obligation to take part in operations of war against their own country," [3] and repeats the prohibition in another article.[4] It also lays upon the occupying forces the duty of respecting " family honour and rights," [5] and insuring " public order and safety." [6] In the face of this the Germans have deported thousands of men and women from Belgium. The number is reported to have by this time exceeded one hundred and twenty thousand. Some of these have been carried off like cattle into Germany, and others into the parts of Northern France in German occupation. Large numbers of them have been set to work in mines, in factories, and in digging trenches under the fire of their own friends and allies.

[1] Article 23 g.
[2] Article 27.
[3] Article 52.
[4] Article 23 h.
[5] Article 46.
[6] Article 43.

Others have been forced to labour in domestic occupations, the young girls in many cases being told off by a refinement of lustful cruelty to be "servants" to German officers in the field. Unwilling workers most of these unfortunate deportees turned out to be; and consequently all the resources of military brutality were employed against them. They were kicked and cuffed, and well-nigh starved, till their strength was broken and not even a German martinet could get any more work out of them. When this stage was reached they were sent home to die. My business in this lecture is to describe for you how a large part of International Law has been overthrown in the course of the present war; but it is hard not to leave the passionless domain of jural discussion, and give vent to the fierce indignation the recital inspires.

The whole tale has not been told, nor can it be told within the limits of a lecture. What has been done in Belgium has been done with equal if not superior brutality in the occupied districts of Northern France. They, too, have been subjected to such enormous requisitions and contributions that the inhabitants have been brought to the verge of starvation. They, too, have seen their most sacred fanes, their most historic monuments, wantonly destroyed. They too have been stripped of a large portion of their inhabitants, who have been most abominably treated and in many cases made to labour on the German lines of defence. And in addition to all this they have undergone an experience that circumstances have not yet enabled the

German commanders to inflict on Belgium.[1] The Teuton hosts were forced in 1917 to evacuate many French towns and villages, and before leaving they devastated the delivered districts with a thoroughness that Attila and his Huns might well have envied. All the resources of science were called in to increase the destructiveness of baffled malice. Even in the first fury of Islamic conquest a line was drawn which it has been reserved for the modern apostles of *Kultur* to pass over. In A.D. 633 Abu-Bekr, the immediate successor of Mahomet, when sending his troops to the conquest of Syria, laid on them these commands, "In your progress through the enemy's land cut down no palms or other fruit trees; destroy not the products of the earth; ravage no fields; burn no dwellings; from the stores of the enemy take only what you need for your wants. Let no destruction be made without necessity. . . . Treat the prisoner and him who surrenders himself to your mercy with pity. . . . Do not disturb the quiet of the monk or hermit, and destroy not their abodes."[2] But the German generals of the year 1917 bade their men destroy universally. They cut down the blossoming orchards. They devastated till not a house, a beast, or a plough was left. They poisoned wells. They ruined and desecrated churches. They even violated the last resting-places of the dead, breaking open the tombs and wantonly scattering their contents. Belgium eagerly awaits the long-deferred hour of her deliverance. When it comes may she be

[1] It was inflicted as fully as time allowed in the Autumn of 1918.

[2] Quoted by Walker, *History of the Law of Nations*, p. 76.

spared the miseries that attended the liberation of parts of Northern France.

So far we have confined our statements to Belgium and Northern France. For these countries our information is voluminous, if not complete. But for other lands it is at present considerably less. We do know, however, that dying babes have been found in hundreds in the arms of dead mothers by the roadsides of Russian Poland, while the mouths of many corpses have contained grass half-devoured in the madness of hunger. We also know that about a third of the population of Serbia has been wiped off the face of the earth by Austrian, German and Bulgarian cruelties, and that in Turkey a campaign of torture and massacre has been carried on against unresisting Armenians with such fiendish thoroughness that only a few hundred thousands of them remain alive.[1] One word from the Kaiser would have stopped the holocaust, but it has never been spoken; and in some localities German agents have egged on the Turkish officials in their hellish work. Moreover by the recent Treaty of Brest-Litovsk which was practically dictated by German diplomatists, Armenian districts, liberated during the war by the arms of Russia, have been handed back to the control of the assassins.[2]

All these things were deemed necessary for the aggrandisement of Germany and the success of her cause,

[1] British Parliamentary Papers, *The Treatment of Armenians in the Ottoman Empire* [Miscellaneous, No. 31 (1916)].

[2] See Article 4.

and have therefore been condoned by her rulers and people. There is no need to deny the assertion of the writers of the Fatherland when they repeat with parrot-like iteration the familiar phrase, "The German conscience is clear." No doubt it is; and by the reality of its ease may be measured the depth of its degradation. It has thoroughly assimilated during the last generation the lesson taught it by Professor Lueder in 1889, "When the circumstances are such that the attainment of the object of the war, and the escape from extreme danger, would be hindered by observing the limitations imposed by the laws of war, and can only be accomplished by breaking through those limitations, the latter is what ought to happen."[1] And in the present war it has happened again and again. We have by no means exhausted in the preceding recital the long catalogue of the horrors which her doctrine of *Kriegsraison* enables Germany to let loose on the world with a conscience that remains clear instead of being haunted by the furies of remorse. The list must be extended still further; and even then it will not be complete; for almost every week adds some new atrocity to those that have gone before.

In 1868 a benighted world accepted the principle that no weapons were to be used which inflicted tortures that were needless for the attainment of the military object of destroying an enemy's fighting efficiency.[2] The German War Book denounced this as mere super-

[1] Holtzendorff, *Handbuch des Völkerrechts,* Vol. IV, p. 254.
[2] Preamble of the Declaration of St. Petersburg.

stition;[1] and early in the War Germany treated it as such, and used a poisonous gas which tortured strong men for three awful days before it finally killed them. She also pumped liquid fire into the ranks of the Allies, though her signature stood with theirs at the bottom of a document which made it illegal "to employ arms, projectiles or material, of a nature to cause superfluous injury."[2] Further, she sent her aircraft to drop bombs indiscriminately on crowded towns and open countrysides irrespective altogether of military objects, though the same document said, "The attack, by any means whatever, of towns, villages, habitations, or buildings which are not defended is forbidden."[3]

Sea warfare is new to Germany; but she has carried into it the same spirit of ruthless and arrogant brutality that marks her war on land. Much of what falls to be said on this subject must come under our next head, which is concerned with neutral rights, or rather with their violation. But here, while we are still considering "frightfulness" as between the belligerents, we must point out that Germany and her subservient allies have worsened and degraded maritime warfare as well as warfare on land. Wherever a German vessel sails the old chivalry of the sea has vanished. To rescue perishing foes; to see in the enemy's sick and wounded brothers in distress and relieve their wants fully and freely, to clasp the hands of valiant prisoners and miti-

[1] See last two paragraphs of the Introduction.
[2] *Hague Règlement,* Art. 23 e.
[3] *Ibid.,* Art. 25.

gate to the utmost the hardships of their captivity, were as proud a boast of the fighting navies of the civilised world as prowess in battle or skill in navigation. But now all this has vanished, at least from one group of combatants. Germany has not only sown the open sea with uncontrolled and unanchored floating mines in flagrant violation of the Hague Convention on the subject,[1] but she has turned the newly-invented submarine into an instrument for inflicting swift, sudden, and violent death on surrendered enemy combatants, and innocent enemy civilians, including even women and children. If any of these last happen to be members of the crew of a British merchantman, or passengers on board her, they are sent to the bottom by the German U-boats with as little compunction as if they had been actively engaged in a naval battle. Nor does the lust for slaughter stop at enemy subjects. Ruthless destruction has from time to time been the lot of neutrals who were exercising their undoubted right to travel on a British vessel of commerce.

Submarine craft are lawful weapons when used against the fighting fleets of an enemy. Warships must rely on their own watchfulness and their own armament to guard them against torpedoes, and the fact that a torpedo is launched from a submerged vessel instead of from a vessel on the surface makes no difference as regards the legality of its use. But as against merchantmen the right of the enemy is capture,

[1] Convention of 1907 on Automatic Submarine Contact Mines, Arts. 1-3.

not destruction, still less destruction without warning, destruction leaving no trace behind. International Law has laid down with exactness the course to be followed when a belligerent cruiser meets an enemy vessel of commerce. It must first signal her to stop, and send on board her an officer with a boat's crew to examine her papers and, if necessary, search her. It may then make a prize of her, and the goods she carries also if they are contraband of war or destined to a blockaded port. Having taken possession of her, and put what is called a prize crew on board of her, it must send her into one of its own ports where a Prize Court is sitting, and this Court must give judgment on the legality of the capture. But the cargo must not be taken out of the captured vessel before she reaches the Prize Court, nor may she be sunk unless it is practically impossible to send her in for adjudication, and even then the safety of her crew and passengers must be provided for. Of all these proceedings the first two only can be carried out by a German submarine. It can signal to an enemy merchantman to stop, and it can send an officer on board to examine papers and search. But it cannot take possession of her for lack of men; nor can it spare a Prize Crew to take her in for adjudication for the same reason. Moreover it dare not attempt to escort her to one of its own ports, because that would mean a voyage on the surface with the almost certain result that it would be captured or destroyed by a British or Allied warship. Being unable, therefore, to fulfil the legal conditions of capture, it cannot lawfully be used for that purpose. Warfare is full of such restraints. The guns you may use against enemy fortifications or enemy troops you may not turn on an open and undefended enemy town. The bombs you may throw into the enemy's trenches you may not drop on his museums or churches. But the German mind does not reason in this way. If a weapon cannot be used for a certain purpose without flagrant breach of the law, then the law must be broken. If only the weapon is sufficiently destructive no limits need be placed on its use. Why should any scruples of humanity and mercy block the way to victory?

We see the same line of reasoning used to justify the dastardly practice of sinking Hospital Ships in spite of the Hague Convention which gives them immunity from attack. The statement that they have been used as transports has been put forward as an excuse. It is absolutely untrue; and one cannot but believe that the German naval authorities knew it to be untrue when they made it. Even had any Allied captain disgraced himself in the manner attributed to us, the Hague Convention for the Adaptation of the Principles of the Geneva Convention to Maritime War provided a remedy. Under it any German cruiser would have the right to search the suspected vessel, and capture it if the commander found his suspicions justified.[1] But German cruisers dare not scour the seas for prizes. Practically the only vessels flying the flag of the Fatherland who can rove in search of victims are the sub-

[1] Articles 4, 8.

marines; and if they cannot capture and take in for adjudication, they can at least destroy without warning, and incidentally massacre. Accordingly they are set to do it; and though sick and wounded men with their noble doctors and devoted nurses are doomed thereby to perish, the foulness of the deed does not make it abhorrent to Germany. Its doers are acclaimed as heroes, and a national subscription is raised to make presentations to them when alive, and erect monuments in their honour after death. The naval artillerymen who turn their guns on open boats full of unarmed sailors and passengers, the cultured officers who first deprive captured foes of their life-belts and then submerge, leaving them to sink in the icy waves, are quite equal to this further occasion. The atrocity of the deed seems to add zest to the doing of it. It is supposed to further the German cause, and that is held to be ample justification.

We now pass on to consider the blow to neutral rights struck by the widespread application of the Doctrine of Reprisals. This presents one of the most dangerous and difficult problems in the whole range of international affairs. It is impossible here to do more than glance at that portion of it which refers to warfare. It is held that when an act that goes beyond the admitted rules and customs of civilised war is committed by one belligerent, the other may retaliate by similar and even more severe acts, in order thereby to make his adversary comply in future with the established practice. As a matter of fact this result is rarely reached. The whole subject is one long illustration of the essential barbarity of war. To begin with the rule of violence is often inaugurated with a light heart. Reprisals are frequently resorted to when the acts alleged against the enemy have not been properly verified, or when the rule alleged to have been broken is one that is by no means accepted on all hands. Constantly they have been excessive in extent or in violence. More often than not the innocent are punished for the guilty. There are numerous instances in which the severities resorted to by way of reprisal have led to increased barbarity on the part of the enemy, instead of bringing about a return to ordinary rules.

Various instances of this have occurred within our own experience in the present war. When the Germans began their illegal submarine warfare early in 1915, we retaliated by placing our U-boat prisoners in stricter captivity than the others. Germany immediately picked out some of the most highly-born and delicately nurtured British officers among her prisoners, and subjected them to such rigorous and cruel confinement that their lives and reason were in danger. In the end we, and not the German naval authorities, gave way, and the U-boat warfare has continued with unabated and even increased barbarity. Again, at a later period in the war one of our air squadrons bombed the open town of Freiburg in Baden in reprisal for German air-raids on London and other centres of civilian population. The result was that we stained our hands in vain with the blood of a few German mothers and babes. Instead of giving up her malpractices, Germany moved into the area we had attacked a large number of our officers whom she held as prisoners. We refrained from further bombing in the district in question for fear of killing our own people, and German air-raids on England have continued ever since, and increased in numbers and severity. In a competition of barbarism the side which is most callous and unscrupulous to start with is bound to win in the end. There are some things which a self-respecting belligerent will not do even to gain a great military advantage, just as a self-respecting man will not forge a cheque to save his business, or a self-respecting woman sell her honour to save her home. The only real remedy is to make it both the right and the duty of the whole civilised world to see that during and after a war all serious allegations of illegal violence are enquired into by an appropriate tribunal, and those found guilty punished according to their deserts, if necessary by the infliction of the death penalty.

But the conduct of Germany in the matter of naval reprisals during the present war surpasses in guilt anything we have hitherto set forth. She has turned upon neutrals, as well as foes, refraining from no means of injuring an enemy, even though her blow against him had to be struck through the sides of a friend. The Autumn of 1917 provided a conspicuous instance. I refer to the affair in the North Sea on October 17, when German cruisers attacked a number of neutral merchantmen under the convoy of the two light British destroyers *Mary Rose* and *Strongbow*. The destroyers fought to the death, but were too weak to drive off the far more heavily armed cruisers. The latter not only set at naught all the chivalry of the sea by refusing to rescue their drowning foes; but smashed with shot and shell the boats of the merchantmen when the unarmed crews strove to escape in them, and finally made off without paying the slightest heed to cries for mercy, leaving the sailors and a few poor women also to perish in the stormy waves. From what I have already said you will understand that they had a right to capture these merchantmen and bring them in for adjudication by a German Prize Court. And the Court would have had a right to condemn them as good prize, since they had accepted enemy convoy. But they had no sort of right to destroy, still less to leave crews and passengers to perish, after killing some by their brutal fusillade.

If you had asked them why they did this murderous deed—for it was nothing less—they would have replied that it was all a matter of reprisal and therefore abundantly justified. Were not these so-called neutrals trading with the English foe? Were they not sailing across a tract of sea which Germany had declared to be a War Zone, and, as such, closed to all traffic? Had they not been warned in German official documents again and again that all who attempted to cross this Zone would be liable to destruction by German mines, and the German U-boats and cruisers who were blockading the British Isles in reprisal for what they deemed the illegal British blockade of the ports and harbours of Germany? This statement assumes, of course, a good deal which the jurists and statesmen of the Fatherland would find it hard to prove. But passing by the legal contentions connected with the so-called British blockade let us take up the question of the German reprisals, since our subject at the present moment is concerned with them. Their violence on this occasion, amounting as it did to actual slaughter, was a fearful outrage upon neutrals. Let Germany punish us, her foes, by reprisals, if she must, since International Law still allows such a sorry travesty of justice. But what vestige of right can she have to destroy Swedish, Danish, and Norwegian life and property because England is carrying on the war against her in a way she has chosen to regard as illegal?

As her reprisals are the climax of brutality, so are her War Zones the climax of illegality. For three centuries International Law has declared that the open ocean is the common highway of the world. All may pass and repass over it on their lawful occasions. Only the pirate is warned off and destroyed, and that because he is the common enemy of mankind. Belligerents may fight on the high seas; and while they are engaged in active operations wise neutrals will keep out of the way lest they should suffer from stray shots. But the moment the action ceases they may resume their voyages, and pass to and fro through what has just been the area of conflict, if their course leads them that way. Belligerents have no more right to close it against neutrals than neutrals have to warn belligerents off it. I am not sure that we are altogether blameless in this matter of War Zones; but at any rate when we have proclaimed one we have indicated safe passages through it; whereas Germany in similar circumstances has threatened to destroy all neutral vessels that attempt to cross it, and has carried out her threat again and again in circumstances of the foulest barbarity.

But she has not been content with this. She must needs add loathsome hypocrisy to callous brutality, and pose before the world as the champion of the freedom of the seas. Yet so brazen is the personation, so clumsy the sham, that one after another in long procession the nations of the world are joining the combination against her. No less than twenty are in it now; and but for fear of the fate of Belgium and Serbia there would be scarce a neutral left. Let the German Armies in the West suffer a signal overthrow, and tortured Holland with outraged Scandinavia will rush to arms, and open to the forces of the Allies a broad way into the heart of the Rhineland. Perhaps then its industrial population will begin to realise the position into which their country has been guided. The lessons of justice and consideration for others, to which they were impervious in the days of their prosperity, may be learnt in the sharp school of adversity. For the welfare of humanity at large, and in the highest interests of the German people as well as our own, we must fight on till the whole system of military rule, with the cult of force and fraud to which it leads, has been discredited and destroyed.

The mental and spiritual condition of Germany to-day is a terrible object-lesson to shew the world what happens when a great people is delivered up, body and soul, to the worship of power, power in the crude form of force embodied in the state and the various organs of its authority. The philosophy of Nietzsche, the historical theories of Treitschke, the politico-biological speculations of Bernhardi, have not been poured forth in vain. A whole nation, full of magnificent enthusiasm for knowledge, marvellous in its erudition, justly renowned throughout the world for its conquests in the domain of science and its skill in many of the arts, has slowly debased itself till it is in danger of becoming a terribly efficient instrument in the destruction of human freedom and the banishment of justice and humanity from international intercourse. The great corrupting influence has been the doctrine that no rule of right, no dictate of mercy and gentleness, must prevail to block the way to any advantage in war, diplomacy or internal administration. Throughout the foregoing recital we have stood aghast at the moral blindness, the perversions in sentiment and atrocities in action, to which it has led. But we found no place in the story for wrongs which did not spring from violations of the laws of war and neutrality. And yet how frequent and how flagrant these have been!—everywhere the same arrogant hectoring of weaker states; everywhere the same double-dealing diplomacy; everywhere the same unscrupulous attempts to set neighbours against one another. Shameless mendacity, unlimited corruption, loathsome treachery—these were the weapons which

Germany stooped to wield. She made use of them in the cabinet and the press, in commerce and industry, and indeed wherever and whenever men came together for mutual intercourse. All the old sanctities were forgotten, all the old restraints ignored. What, for instance, can be more abominable than the use of a diplomatic staff at neutral capitals for the purpose of instigating breaches of the laws of neutrality, and planning outrages on neutral soil against neutral life and property in order to injure a foe? It poisons the whole atmosphere of international intercourse. And yet Germany resorted to it again and again in the United States and other countries, till her own falsity drove them from their neutrality into the ranks of the confederacy against her.

But the diffusion of a pestilential atmosphere may place in great jeopardy those who are fighting the plague. It is necessary for us to be on our guard lest the poison of German political philosophy should infect our own moral being. We are giving our firstborn for the Fatherland's transgression, the fruit of fair English bodies for the sin of the Kaiser's soul. Is not this enough? Must we in addition adopt the accursed doctrine that so-called military necessity justifies the most atrocious deeds? Must we give up our humanity, and the strong sense of justice that has distinguished us for centuries? Hitherto we have been proud to wage this war with clean hands. But now large numbers of us are crying aloud, not only for the bombing of German fortresses, munition works and communications, which is a terrible but lawful operation of war, but for the deliberate slaughter of our enemy's women and babes, which is a ghastly atrocity by whomsoever done and whatsoever be the provocation. In effect we are urged to become murderers, because the Germans have murdered, and to lull our consciences we are told the palpable falsehood that only thus we can stop the atrocities of the enemy. May God keep us from such a degradation of ourselves and our holy cause!

In the course of this lecture I have given ample proof that the International Law of War has been battered into ruins by the German attacks upon it. It needs rebuilding from its foundations if it is ever again to act as a restraint on the worst passions of mankind. Much of the old material is good, but much needs replacing with new. And above all things it is necessary that the doctrine of *Kriegsraison* should be condemned and disavowed. In future the Laws of War must be made to be observed, not to be violated at pleasure by any belligerent who chooses to urge military necessity as his excuse. They must themselves provide for exceptional cases, and tribunals must be established, backed up in the last resort by the whole force of civilised humanity, to punish violations of them by judicial process, and thus rid the world of the legalised iniquity of reprisals. In addition it will be found that the organisation of whole nations for war has made such enormous progress during the present world-conflict that the distinction between combatants and non-combatants bids fair to become obsolete. We will attempt in the next lecture to shew what this implies, and discuss whether remedies can be found for the enormous evils it threatens.

With the hard facts of the present conflict before us it is impossible to escape from another conclusion. We cannot fail to see that the Law of Neutrality is in little better case than the Law of War. The Central Powers have played havoc with it on land and sea; and the Allies have devised restraints on neutral trade which they justify as developments of existing rules rendered necessary by the new conditions of maritime commerce and the lawless conduct of the enemy. We must wait for the calmer days that will come when the war is over before we know how far these justifications will be deemed sufficient by the general consent of the civilised world. But it may be said at once, and without fear of contradiction, that the Allied fleets have been as careful of human life as the Germans have been careless, and have endeavoured by all means in their power to mitigate the hardships caused to neutrals by the fresh rules they have enforced.

But it must not be supposed that because the sketch already drawn reveals widespread ruin, the rest of the picture is equally discouraging. The whole of what is generally called The International Law of Peace stands with little injury. It is true, as we have already seen, that German diplomatists have been revealed as unscrupulous plotters against the well-being of states whose friends they professed to be. But as soon as their misdeeds were discovered the law proved equal to dealing with them. The offending envoys were sent packing with exhilarating celerity. And some of them owed their safe return to the generosity of an opponent they never ceased to vilify. But for British safe-conducts Dr. Dumba and Count Von Bernstorff might still be languishing in some distant land, far away from the governments who have rewarded them and the admirers who deem that they have done yeoman's service to their cause. No one suggests that the Law of Diplomacy needs recasting in consequence of their offences. The Law of Jurisdiction still stands firm on the foundation of territorial sovereignty; while the rules under which states can acquire unoccupied territory, and establish civilised government in it, may perhaps require development, but call for little alteration.

It may be urged that the downfall of a large portion of a building must weaken the rest. But this is not a truth of universal application. It is possible that the part destroyed was kept in position by the strength of the remainder, which may stand firmer than before when released from the strain. In any case there is the probability that the crash may lead to a rebuilding on better lines and with more carefully chosen materials. All depends on the value of the edifice in the eyes of those who own it, and in the energy and resource they display in their efforts after restoration. In the case before us it is clear that civilised humanity does not desire to destroy International Law, but rather to improve and strengthen it; for nearly the whole world has armed, or is arming, in its defence.

* LECTURE V.

THE CONDITIONS OF RECONSTRUCTION.

Those who have at heart the welfare of their kind, and have not fallen victims to the German heresy of the absolute right to domination possessed by the superman and the super-state, must draw but one conclusion from the facts I have laid before you. They cannot fail to see that the work of building up the shattered edifice of International Law concerns the whole of civilised humanity. Neutrals as well as belligerents are affected to an enormous extent by many of the incidents of the present struggle. It is not a question of loss or inconvenience to a few traders here and there, but of widespread national distress. Whole populations, like those of Holland and Norway, have been reduced to acute discomfort, if not actual want; and whole classes, such as seamen, have been placed in peril of their lives. War as it is waged to-day means for many neutrals at least as much danger and distress

* The victories which secured the triumph of the cause upheld in these pages were won while this Lecture and the next were in the press. Recent events have thus strengthened the conclusions reached beforehand. It is, however, necessary to ask the reader to alter a good many assertions from the present to the past tense, and regard as affirmations several statements that are set forth in the text in the language of anticipation and probability.

as falls to the average civilian in the belligerent countries. It is essential therefore that neutral states should have a voice in shaping the better order that is to render such conditions impossible in the future. And this is the more necessary because of three great changes that have come into general notice since July, 1914, though their beginnings can be traced back to earlier years.

The first of these events is the practical obliteration of the all-important distinction between combatants and non-combatants. The division of the people of a belligerent state into these two great classes, and the grant to the second of far more favourable treatment than is accorded to the first, was not embodied in the Law of War till comparatively recent times. The distinction slowly emerged during the century after Grotius, and became one of the most humanising influences to be found in the whole history of mankind. In the earliest days of recorded history either slaughter or slavery was the lot of conquered populations.[1] As time went on the lives of the peaceful inhabitants of an enemy's country were spared, though they were still led into captivity. Then special classes were left unmolested, some on account of the harmlessness of their lives, and others because of the sacredness of their functions. Among those whom it was deemed unlawful to slay or enslave were women, children, husbandmen, artisans and ministers of religion.[2] Finally, as the

[1] Grotius, *De Jure Belli ac Pacis,* Bk. III, Ch. IV.

[2] *Ibid.,* Bk. III, Ch. XI, §§ 9-12.

result of generations of progress in the direction of mercy, a great generalisation was made, and all non-combatants were deemed to be exempt from the worst severities of warfare. They were to be protected from outrage and allowed to go about their ordinary avocations, as long as they sent no military information to their own side, submitted quietly to the control of the invaders, and neither planned nor executed any warlike operations against them. The principles thus briefly sketched were embodied in the Military Code annexed to the Hague Convention on the Laws and Customs of War on Land.[1] Its rules represent the highest point to which the tide of humanity has yet risen in military matters. We have already seen in Lecture IV, how shamefully many of them have been violated during the present war by the invading armies of the Central Powers, and what terrible treatment has often been meted out to the inhabitants of what are called occupied districts. But I feel bound to add that the setback to progress thus indicated does not spring entirely from the demoralisation of Germany. It is partly due to the use without stint or limit of all the highly developed power of the modern state for military purposes. Before 1914 the organisation of whole nations for war had made great strides. Compulsory military service had taken within its net large, and ever larger, portions of the manhood of the leading states of the world. A regular cult of the sword as the great teacher of duty and discipline had sprung up. Germany

[1] See Articles 4, 23, 44-52.

led the way in both the theory and the practice of this new religion. Other countries followed, till at last over nearly all Europe, and wide tracts beyond its borders, practically the whole male population was trained for service in the field. But during the present war matters have been carried much further. The womanhood of the belligerent nations has followed in the footsteps of their manhood, and even the children are entering on the same path. We are constantly told that those who make munitions of war at home are doing as valuable service as those who fire them out of guns and rifles at the front. Undoubtedly this is true; and the same principle applies to many others besides munition workers. A very large proportion of these patriotic toilers are women. And further, a considerable amount of war-service is done by children, as for instance in gathering crops, collecting materials, and distributing literature. How is it possible in the face of such facts to maintain the distinction between combatants and non-combatants? But what is to take its place? Is the clock of progress to go back three hundred years, and the track of invading armies to be again marked by promiscuous destruction? Are women to be made into prisoners of war at the best, and at the worst violated and slaughtered? Shall children be gathered wholesale into internment camps, and distributed thence into industrial and domestic slavery? The problem is terribly real. It arises from the very nature of the case. The boasted modern organisation of whole nations, and not merely their armed forces, for war, has provided the world with as fruitful a hotbed of moral and jural difficulties as ever confronted men of thought in their studies or men of action in the field. Frankly, I see no way to deal with it, and at the same time preserve the old humanities and chivalries of war. The only real remedy is to remove the soil from which the evils spring. No half-measures can be effective; and it is impossible to go back to the conditions of fifty years ago. But we may go forward. The world can and must be organised for peace, and not for war.

We must now consider the second of those great and recent changes that cry aloud to civilised humanity, and lay on it the task of saving the world from ruin. It is concerned with the sea and its use. By the adoption of their unrestricted U-boat warfare the Germans practically made war on all the commercial shipping of the world, in order to strike what they fondly believed would be a mortal blow at England. They sought, but in vain, to prevent the coming of food and raw material to her ports, and the transport of men and munitions from them to the various fronts. This war of theirs on shipping meant a war on shipmen also. They cannot, as we have seen,[1] capture the vessels in the only lawful way, which is scrupulously tender of human life. But they can sink them, and in so doing they often sink those who man them as well. It is calculated that since the war began over 12,000 neutral mariners have been sent to their doom in this way. The

[1] See pp. 107-109.

wounded tiger in the jungle reserves its spring for the hunters and beaters. The German tiger of the seas turns in its blood-guilty rage on unarmed men, and defenceless women and their babes.

This gross and wicked illegality is accomplished by another just as illegal, and more likely, because it is not at first sight so inhuman, to be allowed to pass without general reprobation. I allude to the attempt to deprive neutrals of their ancient and undoubted right to traverse freely the open seas of the world, as long as they observe the rules set up between states for the regulation of oceanic commerce in time of war, such for instance as that which prohibits on pain of capture the sea-carriage of contraband to a belligerent. In remote antiquity those who thought about the sea at all seem to have regarded it as being like the air a gift of nature to all mankind. When the Roman lawyers attempted to give legal form to current theories, they declared that it was one of the *res communes*, the things common to all which anyone could use but no one acquire as property.[1] But if we follow the scanty guidance contained in the earliest records we possess we find that the sea, as Sir Henry Maine has said, "was common only in the sense of being universally open to depredation."[2] When the power of Rome was at its height vigorous measures were taken against the pirate fleets, and the Mediterranean was in reality free to peaceful merchantmen. But with the break-up

[1] Justinian, *Institutes*, Bk. II, Tit. I, § 1.
[2] *International Law*, p. 76.

of the Empire the old conditions returned. The sight of a sail at sea caused terror to the inhabitants of coastal districts. Bitter experience taught them to regard it as the bearer of lawless and cruel men, who would plunder and destroy their homes, slaughter all who resisted, and carry off the survivors into slavery. The barbarous custom of wrecking arose quite as much from the promptings of self-defence as from cupidity. Great secular rulers and good Popes alike made war upon it, but it did not even begin to die out till the mediæval order developed from the chaos of the dark ages, and the seas became again to some extent highways of commerce. With the revival of maritime traffic there set in a great movement towards the assertion of proprietary rights in the seas and territorial jurisdiction over them. The Baltic was claimed by Denmark and Sweden jointly; the Northern Seas from Stadland in Norway to Cape Finisterre in Spain by England; the Adriatic by Venice; and the Gulf of Genoa by Genoa. These are but examples, not an inclusive list. Such claims were often challenged by other powers who disputed their validity and desired to exercise authority themselves. But few, if any, in mediæval times objected on principle to sovereignty over the open ocean. The Prince who possessed a sea had to "keep" that sea, that is to say he was held bound to protect those who sailed over it from unlawful depredations. As long as he did this with any kind of efficiency he was regarded more as a benefactor than a usurper. His dominion was not held to justify the exclusion of vessels of other nations, though sometimes tolls were levied on them, and licences to fish sold to them. The movement of thought in the middle ages seems to have run strongly in the direction of what is called *mare clausum;* and apparently no sense of grievance arose to counteract it till after the discovery of America, and the opening out of the sea-route to India from Western Europe round the Cape of Good Hope. Then Portugal claimed the Indian Ocean, and Spain the Pacific, and each endeavoured to keep the vessels of other powers out of its sea domain. Naturally the rising maritime states resisted. Their strong desire to share in the wealth of the Orient and the New World prompted them to challenge the claim to exclude them from the waters which led to what were deemed the golden lands beyond. They cast about for a legal theory to justify their position, and found it in the old doctrine of the Roman Jurists that the sea was incapable of permanent appropriation, while its use was common to all. Hence arose towards the end of the sixteenth and the beginning of the seventeenth century the great *Mare Clausum* and *Mare Apertum* controversy, with Grotius as the most prominent representative of the new notions. When once it was recognised that maritime states must have rights of ownership and control over the waters that wash their shores and the gulfs and bays that penetrate into their land territory, the victory of the advocates of *Mare Apertum* was rapid and complete. The theory that the open sea was the common highway of all mankind, and therefore free to all for passage and commerce, was so obviously fitted for the new era of trans-oceanic trade, and so clearly beneficial to the human race, that it met with general acceptance when modified so as to provide for the exigencies of national defence. Hence it came to pass that in the early days of modern International Law a jurisprudence of the ocean was rapidly developed. Its foundation principle was that the open seas of the world were absolutely free from the dominion and control of any state or group of states, but could be used by each and all for their lawful occasions, without any further let or hindrance than that which arose from the obligation to respect the corresponding rights of others. Pirates, as enemies of the human race, could be captured and punished by any who were strong enough to seize them. The operations of war were reckoned among the lawful occasions for which the open sea might be used, but no belligerent could permanently occupy its waters for his warlike purposes, just as no trading state could fence off a portion of the ocean for its traffic alone. The right of blockade may possibly be regarded as an exception to the rule against permanent and exclusive use of an element common to all. But, if so, it is the only one; and the right to warn off vessels from the neighbourhood of the blockaded ports ceases the moment the blockade ceases. The doctrine that the high seas of the globe are open to all in war as well as in peace has stood firm for centuries on the rock of universal consent.

But it is in jeopardy now. New modes of warfare

have arisen, and new means of transmitting information. The result has been a tendency on the part of belligerents to encroach on neutral rights in order to utilise these things in their own interests and turn them against their adversaries. We have before us a small extension of belligerent authority as against neutrals in 1904, and an enormous inroad on neutral rights about ten years afterwards. The second followed the first largely because what was done on the former occasion received no international regulation and limitation. The chain of events began when in the Russo-Japanese War a vessel which was undoubtedly neutral was equipped for wireless telegraphy, and used by a correspondent of the *Times* for the transmission to his paper of intelligence concerning the doings of the fighting fleets. Here was a new case, and one which obviously required some development of belligerent control; for it is clear that the smallest lack of discretion or good faith might have resulted in the gift of valuable information to one side or the other in the war.[1] Each belligerent dealt with the matter in its own way. The Russian Admiral threatened to treat as a spy the correspondent who initiated the plan; and the Japanese authorities warned him off a certain portion of the high seas. Clearly he was no spy; for he acted openly, and the essence of espionage is secrecy. But the possible dangers to belligerents that lurked in such proceedings as his were sufficient to justify some restriction of his

[1] Higgins, *War and the Private Citizen*, pp. 89-112; Lawrence, *War and Neutrality in the Far East*, Chap. V.

common law right of free navigation. In the Proceedings of the United States Naval War College for 1904 will be found a carefully reasoned statement as to what the restrictions should be.[1] Unfortunately no convention embodying them has been negotiated between states. Belligerents were left free to be mild or severe, reasonable or unreasonable, as seemed good to them when the emergency arose, with the result that in 1915 a particularly arrogant and unscrupulous belligerent ignored neutral rights entirely. Very early in the world-war Germany laid mines in the North Sea and the Atlantic highway round the North of Ireland. Some of them were unanchored and certainly did not fulfil the requirement of being " so constructed as to become harmless an hour at most after those who laid them lost control over them."[2] Great Britain was unwilling to resort to mines at all, and refrained from making use of them till several merchant vessels, neutral as well as British, had been destroyed, and no less than sixty persons of neutral nationality drowned. When at last we retaliated in the Autumn of 1914 we refrained entirely from the use of unanchored mines, and warned mariners of the position of our fields of anchored mines, according to the terms of the Hague Convention that deals with the subject.[3] It has been suggested that Germany was free to disregard this Convention because Montenegro, one of the belligerents, had not

[1] See pp. 112-116.

[2] Hague Convention of 1907 on *Automatic Submarine Contact Mines*, Art. 1.

[3] See Article 3.

signed it, and its seventh article laid down that its provisions were applicable "only if all the belligerents" were parties to it. This excuse, if it is seriously put forward, sets up a most minute technical point against a plain precept of humanity. Whether or not it is good in the forum of law, the fact that it is relied on is enough to ensure condemnation in the forum of conscience. In that exalted court the plea that the Convention need not be observed because a mere atom of a state which does not possess a single sea-going ship neglected to sign it would meet with nothing but contempt and indignation.

We have just seen that during the last few years there has been a general neglect on the part of the whole body of civilised states to define clearly the exceptional circumstances under which belligerents might limit the free navigation of the seas in time of war, and prescribe the exact nature of the limitations which could be permitted. It stands to reason that such neglect would be exploited to the full by a power which in order to gain an advantage in war violated a Convention regarded even by its authors as pitiably weak in the restraints it put on the employment of submarine mines. Accordingly we find that Germany, in retaliation for our attempt to prevent goods from abroad from reaching her across the ocean, carried still further the lawless attacks on human life she had initiated by her promiscuous use of mines. In February, 1915, she declared the sea for some distance round the British Isles to be what she called indifferently a Naval War

Zone or a Barred Zone, and we will call a War Zone. By this she meant that British and Allied vessels traversing the area in question would be liable to destruction at any time by her submarines, and in addition that neutral merchantmen would be exposed to similar danger. At the end of January, 1917, she multiplied her War Zones, extending them to the Atlantic and the Mediterranean, and at the same time withdrew the concession she had made to the United States in the previous May to the effect that American vessels should not be sunk without warning and without opportunity of escape being given to those on board them. For the future there was to be no faltering. From February 1, 1917, she intended to prevent by force navigation to and from the coasts of her enemies. To quote her own words, "all ships met within the Zone will be sunk."[1]

This is what is meant by unrestricted U-boat warfare. As we all know it brought the United States into the fight early in the following April; and neither America nor the powers associated with her in the struggle are likely to end it without obtaining the fullest security against the repetition in future of such murderous attacks. We have previously discussed them from the point of view of a proper regard for human life. Now I want to point out that legally they are fatal to what has been regarded for about three centuries as one of the fundamental rights of civilised mankind. What becomes of the time-honoured doc-

[1] German Memorandum of January 31, 1917.

trine that the open seas of the world are free for all to traverse on their lawful occasions, if any belligerent who can make a vast area of them dangerous is allowed to reserve it as a sort of sea-province of his own, and warn neutrals off on pain of death? A more manifest usurpation it is impossible to conceive. And where is it to end? If neutrals submit to it, they must be content in future to navigate the ocean by the gracious permission of warring states. Their old right becomes a privilege, granted or withheld at the will of others. War is installed as Lord Paramount of the world; and Peace stands humbly in the background ready to pick up with effusive gratitude such morsels as the real master of God's earth may throw to her. Not the least of the services which the United States have done to mankind during their national existence was rendered when they threw down the gage of battle to a power whose monstrous War Zones robbed civilisation of one of its most essential means of existence. Let us hope that when success has crowned their efforts, they and we, and the nations allied with us, will see to it that the revised International Code which will assuredly come into being not only re-enacts the old right in the plainest terms, but also provides means for enforcing it promptly against all gainsayers.

The third of the great changes which have become apparent to all the world since the outbreak of the present war is concerned with the air. Its conquest was a triumph of scientific knowledge and mechanical skill. But instead of being used for the welfare of humanity it was at once pressed into the service of destruction. Germany, as we have seen in the fourth Lecture, led the way in its perversion. The other belligerents have followed, till now there seems a prospect that new and more terrible miseries will be added to the already superabundant horrors of war. Few of us, I think, yet realise the nature and extent of the destruction that may be wrought on the earth from the air in the next great war. What belligerent countries now suffer is a mere trifle in comparison with it. States will guard their air-frontiers with organised air-forces, as they now guard their land-frontiers with armies. Great battles will take place in the space above the borders, and the vanquished will have to suffer the horrors of air-invasion. What these will be no tongue or pen can describe. For one air-raid to-day there will be scores in a few years' time; for one aeroplane, hundreds; for one airman, thousands. Squadron after squadron will come over in wave after wave, and each will cut a broad swath of destruction across the invaded land. Town after town will be subjected to continuous bombardment on one excuse or another, till nothing will be left but masses of smoking ruins. The capital and the more important military or manufacturing centres will probably be protected by gigantic bomb-proof structures; but the whole country cannot be thus roofed with steel. It will be turned into one vast Gehenna, loathsome with the shattered corpses of unarmed civilians, and smoking with the lurid mirk of a thousand incendiary fires. To this we shall come within a few more years, if mankind is so callous or so hopeless as to take no precautions against it. Writing in 1908, I made a vain attempt to awaken rulers and shipping interests to the dangers threatening life and property in any maritime war of the immediate future, in spite of the humanitarian aspirations so freely set forth and so feebly translated into rules at the Hague Conference of the previous year. After reviewing various questions in some detail, I summed up in the words, "There is no escape from the conclusion that in any war which covered a considerable portion of the world's seas, and was fought out to a finish by powerful navies, there would be wholesale slaughter of non-combatants, the majority of whom would probably be neutral. As for property, it would be destroyed right and left, in spite of all the immunities which have been secured for neutral trade within the last century."[1] No one took the slightest notice of what I said. Chambers of Commerce were too much occupied with championing all the old severities of naval warfare to make any attempt to realise the new dangers that threatened international trade. Politicians were so full of zeal for the discomfiture of their political foes that they had no energy to spare for safeguarding humanity from freshly devised horrors. I was a voice crying in the wilderness, a mere writer on International Law and therefore, of course, a feckless hair-splitter or a dreamy cosmopolitan. I should not expect any better

[1] Lawrence, *International Problems and Hague Conferences*, pp. 175-176.

fate to-day but for the fact that the imagination of the public has been excited by all that appertains to the new art of flying. What the student of international affairs cannot hope to do by himself may be accomplished with the potent aid of the engineer and the novelist. And when once people are thoroughly awake to the immense possibilities for evil as well as for good contained in aircraft, they may be induced to combat the former as well as develop the latter.

To assist the awakening process let us try to bring into one focus our recent conclusions. We have seen that in modern warfare nations are organised for mutual destruction far more completely than they have ever been before, vast stretches of open ocean are withdrawn from peaceful uses and reserved for belligerent operations, and from the air we breathe the weapons of death are showered down upon us in ever-increasing abundance. It follows from the first of these developments that the comparatively merciful treatment granted for centuries to non-combatants will rapidly vanish, from the second that the seas will no longer be free in the sense that all may traverse them on their legitimate business, and from the third that destruction of life and the means of living will be more indiscriminate, more complete, and more widespread than it has ever been before, even in the darkest of the dark ages. All this, it seems to me, is bound to take place quite apart from any special lawlessness or cruelty in one or more of the belligerents. It is inherent in the nature of the case. War has made a conscription of all the arts and sciences, and pressed them without stint into its service. To do so it had to break through many wholesome restraints, and violate many time-honoured sanctities. But this having been accomplished the consequences I have sketched will inevitably follow, unless mankind at large makes a general effort in the opposite direction. To Germany belongs by far the greater portion of the discredit. She has not only developed a reasoned theory of the State and of War, under which all these things were certain to take place; but she has led the way in their inauguration knowingly, thoroughly, gleefully. Her guilt will be shared by the other nations, if they make no attempt to stem the tide of horror and ruin. History shews that when once new means of destruction gain a foothold in warfare they come to stay until they are superseded by other and more effective weapons. Moral considerations may for a long time prevent their adoption; but I doubt whether any of them, when received into general use, have ever been abandoned owing to conscientious scruples. We must make up our minds to the employment in the warfare of the future of high explosives, flame-jets, poisonous gases, submarines, bombing aeroplanes, and all the rest of the devilish enginery with which we are now familiar. Moreover the potency of science in destruction will increase with the progress of invention, and this we cannot stop, even if we foolishly wished to do so. What we can do is to diminish and finally destroy the medium in which science works for the torture and ruin of mankind. There is no reason in the nature of things why states should settle their differences by a resort to force. Once it was the proud boast of every freeman that he redressed his grievances by the might of his own strong arm. But in the end the method of judicial trial proved far more satisfactory, and secured universal adoption among civilised communities, faulty though it often was in its early days, and far from perfect as its results sometimes are even now. Why should not national quarrels be decided in the same way? No doubt there are difficulties, and some of them are very great. But they can be overcome if mankind is in earnest, though nothing less than a strong, general and persistent determination to achieve the end in view will suffice. When every man was his own guardian and his own avenger, it was difficult to get him to give up his barbaric freedom, and become an unit in a society where law took the place of naked force, and reason superseded passion. The process took ages, but it was completed at last; and now in every civilised state it is an offence visited with severe punishment to do what was done as a matter of course in the old days and, in graphic popular phrase, take the law into one's own hands. Already states have constituted a society, as I shewed in the second Lecture. If they willed, they could become a society organised for the purpose of administering justice between its members. At the close of the present war civilised humanity must decide whether to take a big step forwards towards international peace and brotherhood or stagger back to barbarism amid ever-increasing horrors. The most fateful moment in the world's history since the birth of the babe of Bethlehem will have arrived. The great choice of which Lowell sings will be put to mankind:—

Once to every man and nation comes the moment to decide
In the strife of Truth with Falsehood for the good or evil side!
Some great cause, God's new Messiah, offering each the bloom or blight,
Parts the goats upon the left hand, and the sheep upon the right,
And the choice goes by for ever 'twixt that darkness and that light.

But on this occasion no individual, no national, determination will be sufficient. The matter is one for the human race as a whole. It need not be unanimous, but it must come to a definite conclusion. Hesitation and delay will amount to the same thing as a deliberate choice of evil; for the old bad system of constant distrust and incessant preparation for mutual destruction will still remain, and grow worse and worse as the years roll by. But if the alternative of light and good is taken, then there must be a united effort to realise all that such a splendid decision implies. The opportunity will be before us soon, and there must be no paltering with it.

The very magnitude of the present evil will secure to us such possibilities of reformation as have never before presented themselves. Hitherto the nations have moved in a vicious circle. No single one among them has dared to disarm and trust to neighbourliness and just dealing for peace and security, because by so doing it would render itself helpless against the others and invite attack by its defenceless condition. The most unscrupulous and ambitious powers would have the rest at their mercy, and the arrogant, not the meek, would inherit the earth. But the measures resorted to for protection were made the excuse for further armaments on the part of those who desired to fish in troubled waters. Thus the evil grew not only through the action of those states who saw their advantage in it, but also through the precautions taken in order to foil their designs. Nothing can prove efficacious against it but a general agreement to organise the Society of Nations for peace instead of war; and this was impossible in the state of mind prevailing till lately among many peoples. But the experience of the last few years has been so awful that, for the time being at any rate, the most militant have been sobered by it. Moreover the war is a world-war, which means, among other things, that the majority of civilised states are parties to it, and must therefore come together by their plenipotentiaries to negotiate the terms of peace. Not only will the assembly be representative of all the belligerent nations, but it is quite possible that important neutrals will in some capacity, though not as principals, be admitted to it. In any case it will be a Congress unlike any other that has ever assembled to end a war. It will be unique in the number of states represented at it, and unique in the chastened mood of all the parties to it, not excepting the bleeding and exhausted victors. Its spirit will be the spirit of the civilised world and its decisions will be the decisions of mankind. In it and by means of it, the vicious circle may be broken, and the peoples of the earth set free from its accursed domination. Never before has a similar opportunity arisen, and if it is allowed to slip mankind may never have another. To let it pass would be one of the most grievous sins against light the world has ever witnessed. Unless the human race has lost all vision of justice and brotherhood, all care for peace and security, and all love for what is beautiful and holy, it will strive as it has never striven before so to organise the Society of Nations that for the future war will be difficult, if not impossible. Given a few more years of such waste, destruction and cruelty as we have recently endured, and civilisation will be at its last gasp. The world cannot afford to wait for the slow evolution of a remedy, especially as it seems probable that warfare, if left to the gradual development of customary observances, will grow in severity rather than in mercy. Spontaneous submission to German domination is unthinkable; and surrender, if brought about by force, would inaugurate universal slavery, not the willing obedience of free peoples to laws of their own imposing. It follows, therefore, that the general and express consent of states is the only possible agent of immediate reforn. By this means mankind must establish a new and better international order. There is no other way. It has been trodden already, as we saw in the third Lecture, at the Hague Conferences of 1899 and 1907. It can be used again without any break in the continuity of international development, and we can learn by the experience already gained to make it a much more efficient instrument of progress than it was before.

As a first step in the organisation of the world for peace rather than for war the duty of helping to enforce International Law must be laid on all states. If they are not willing to shoulder the burden, it is useless to go further. The world must be left to rush headlong to perdition in its blindness, and lack of devotion to the common welfare. The plans for a fresh struggle will be laid on the day when the present conflict ends. All the wealth and all the mental equipment which should have gone into the work of social and international reconstruction will go instead into preparations for mutual slaughter. The air will be alive with fleets of war-planes, and the sea above and beneath the surface will be filled with new and more terrible instruments of destruction. On land fresh weapons, more powerful explosives, more diabolical methods of maiming and torture, will constantly come into being. From such a prospect even Germany might shrink. But the willing assumption by all nations of the obligation to restrain and punish peace-breakers is the price to be paid for deliverance. Nor is it burdensome when compared with the benefits it will purchase. In fact it would involve far smaller sacrifices than the condition of armed peace varied occasionally by devasting wars which is the only practical alternative. The conviction that in states a similar obligation, resting on individual citizens, is the only real security for justice between man and man and the safety of life and limb, has been growing steadily from age to age. To-day the strongest individualist would not dream of going back to primitive conditions of chaotic disorder and almost unbridled anarchy. The self-restraint and corporate action necessary for the establishment of a better order have become a second nature to most of us, and made the task of maintaining and improving it so easy that all we have to do is to pay our police-rates cheerfully, and support the authorities in bringing the whole weight of the public forces to bear on those who defy the law. There is nothing to shew that this state of affairs could not be reproduced in the Society of Nations, if civilised mankind willed it. As a recent writer has well said, " Personal safety and social justice depend upon the practice of mutual protection, and it may be confidently asserted that national safety and international peace must be based upon that same principle." [1]

Undoubtedly the peaceful life and general content with the law and its administration that are such marked features in all well-governed national communities would not be attained at one bound in the community of states under a reorganised international order. Neither, on the other hand, would the transition

[1] A. J. Jacobs, *Neutrality versus Justice*, p. 13.

from the rule of force to the rule of right be so long or so difficult a process in the Society of Nations as it is proved to be in the Society of Individuals. The discipline mankind has gone through in the latter will fit it for the quicker and better performance of its work in the reform of the former. The statesmen of to-day, even though they may display all the shortcomings it is the fashion to impute to most of them, are at any rate much more restrained and cultured beings than were Frankish chiefs or Saxon thanes, and the peoples for whom they speak have learnt in the course of centuries to appreciate the benefits of peace and stability. For some time past we have lived under an international order corresponding roughly to the internal order which subsisted for centuries within the older State-communities. Courts were gradually established to try disputes between individuals and inflict punishment for crime, while the old right of private vengeance was not at first absolutely abolished, but allowed only under strict regulations. Similarly nations have had their Arbitral Tribunals, and have resorted to them with increasing frequency; but they have not yet given up the right of making war at their own will and pleasure, though in waging it they have accepted more or less completely certain restraints which are embodied in what we call the laws of war. The Society of Nations is now in the same condition as the Society of Individuals was in England in the time of Alfred the Great, who provided in his Dooms that the kindred of a murdered man should wait for seven days before they attempted to slay the murderer, and if he consented within that time to make the money compensation which was the legal satisfaction for his crime, he was not to be attacked at all. In other words it is just beginning to emerge from barbarism. But as individuals were in time completely converted to orderly ways, and consented to laws which made penal that resort to the blood feud which was once the proud privilege of every freeman, so it may come to pass that states shall soon agree to put under a ban as enemies of the common weal those of their number who resort to war instead of to International Courts of Arbitration or Committees of Conciliation. There is nothing utopian in the suggestion. If acted on, it would but carry one step further a process of evolution which has been worked out already in its earlier stages in close resemblance to the historical development of civilised society within progressive states. There is one great lesson which surely must have been burnt into the mind and conscience of humanity by the terrible experience of the last few years. It is that each nation must not only obey the rules of International Law itself, but help to enforce them on others. When once this lesson has been learnt, it ought not to pass the wit of man to devise ways and means for carrying it into practice. We will venture to make a few suggestions as to the methods that might be followed, bearing in mind that those are most likely to meet with acceptance that grow naturally out of institutions and arrangements already in use among the powers in their mutual intercourse.

We may take for granted that after the war a great assemblage of plenipotentiaries will come together to settle the final conditions on which the struggle will be ended. This will involve much discussion and will take a long time. Now a peace by negotiation is sometimes denounced as an unpatriotic surrender of high purposes and noble aims, and sometimes exalted as a triumph of reason and morality over passion and injustice. Both attitudes are mistaken; for in truth the phrase describes the means used, not the result attained. A peace dictated by a conqueror to a thoroughly beaten foe might conceivably be just and even generous. A peace reached by diplomatic bargaining might be unjust and sordid to the last degree. The antithesis frequently proclaimed between peace by negotiation and peace by constraint is false. Its constant repetition by great masses of mankind serves only to shew that most of us are slaves of *formulæ*. Negotiation there must be when a score or more of states, including all the Great Powers of the World, have been at war for years. In such circumstances it is an impossibility that any one of them, however strong and victorious, can dictate its will in every particular; and even if it could, negotiations would still be necessary in order to correlate its objects with those of its allies, and put them all into proper diplomatic phraseology. For reasons that will be given immediately I find myself in complete agreement with those who urge that no formal Peace Congress should be summoned till the enemy is ready to accept our primary demands of restitution and reparation, respect for international right and security for future good behaviour. But how is this to be known without some interchange of views, however informal, beforehand; and when it is known, how are the details of the settlement to be worked out without much discussion and a good deal of give and take? And what is this but negotiation? The idea of a peace without it is about as sensible as that of a loaf without flour or a debate without speech. But just as the mere presence of flour does not secure that a loaf is good, and the mere use of speech does not of necessity make a debate eloquent and ennobling, so the mere fact that negotiation has taken place will not guarantee that the terms of peace are just and righteous. Neither on the other hand will it imply that they must be unsatisfactory. It simply means that a necessary instrument has been used. The goodness or badness of the result depends on the spirit in which the use is made.

But while whatever peace is reached must be a peace of negotiation, there is all the difference in the world between a peace reached by a process of bargaining and a peace enshrining the views and ideals of one side or the other in the struggle. The former suits what may be called business disputes, as when states have gone to war for territory or economic advantages. The latter is the only tolerable solution when the war is a war of principles involving the deepest convictions, the most cherished ideals, the most passionate emotions of the combatants. This is the case in the present world-conflict. I do not often feel moved to express approval of any of the Kaiser's utterances. But he seems to me to have spoken with true insight when on June 15, 1918, on the thirtieth anniversary of his accession, he declared that the war he is now waging was "a struggle of two world-views which were wrestling with one another," and added that either "the German views . . . must be upheld, or the Anglo-Saxon principles . . . must be victorious." Though when he went on to describe the German principles as "right, freedom, honour and morality," and the Anglo-Saxon principles as "the idolatry of Mammon," one can only regard his words as a glaring instance of that colossal self-deception and arrogant presumption which looks upon everything German as necessarily good, and everything opposed to Germany's acts and designs as in consequence utterly evil. The world outside the Kaiser's realm has formed a very different judgment. It holds, as he does, that two incompatible ideals are striving for the mastery. But it believes that in this great battle of the nations the Allies are the champions of political freedom and international righteousness, even though each one of them may have some spots on its record in these respects. A German triumph would assuredly result in the enthronement of autocracy in the sphere of internal affairs, and the exaltation of brute force as the determining factor in all transactions between states. "There is no International Law," said William II to Mr. Gerard, the American Ambassador, and his Chancellor endorsed the anarchical sentiment. "There is no need of any," say thousands of his subjects, seeing that victorious Germany will settle all external questions according to her views of her own interests, which other nations will in time come to see must be theirs also.

When we consider not only German aims, but also the brutal and crooked means used to attain them, we shall see that the real struggle is between progress and reaction, right and wrong, the realisation of the brotherhood of nations or the consummation of their slavery to one great super-state and its satellites. For nothing less is the field set: for no smaller issue is the battle joined. One result only will save civilisation, and that is the defeat and overthrow of the German military system. This, therefore, we must strain every nerve to accomplish, failing repentance, of which there are no signs in the utterances of German rulers or the temper of the German people. High-sounding talk there is in abundance, and constant professions of willingness to negotiate, but no frank acceptance of the sole conditions of a righteous and abiding peace. Instead we have vague *formulæ* accepted "in principle," only to be circumvented and discarded in practice whenever Germany is able to force a treaty on a beaten and humiliated foe. The German spirit remains the same throughout; and till it has been purged by the stern discipline of military overthrow there is no prospect of change. For this cause we of the Allied nations must steel ourselves to agonise and persevere. To patch up a settlement at once would be false to the high aims with which we entered the war, and treason to those who have given their lives to safeguard liberty and enthrone justice. Moreover it would be fatal to the cause of peace, which can prevail only by the destruction of the citadel of force and unright. No people would benefit thereby more than the Germans themselves. They can be brought to a better mind and made to respect the claims of human brotherhood by the discovery that war is not a profitable national industry, and apparently in no other way. America is thoroughly awake to this great truth. And now that she has joined us with all her vast resources we should indeed be traitors to the cause of righteousness if we slackened our efforts, and gave new life to the deceit, the cruelty, the limitless ambition of the enemy. If we give way now, in what respect are we better than the ancient Hebrew faint-hearts of whom the terrible words were written, " Curse ye Meroz, saith the angel of the Lord; curse ye bitterly the inhabitants thereof; because they came not to the help of the Lord, to the help of the Lord against the mighty "?

But there is little fear of such a pitiful surrender. Our hearts are high and our resolution unbroken. We are beginning to find out that Germany is not invincible. The crowning victory for which she flouted public law and outraged the dictates of humanity still eludes her grasp. She sold her soul for a price which, thank God, remains unpaid. And now, deprived of the speedy triumph on which she counted, she is struggling on with alternations of success and defeat. But both alike are slowly sapping her strength, till at length, if only the Allies maintain their dauntless courage and steadfast brotherhood, she must stagger in ever-increasing weakness to the inevitable doom. All the atrocities of military "frightfulness," all the resources of bad faith, all the shifts and subterfuges of insincere diplomacy will have been tried in vain. The wages of sin will be paid in the death of the abominable system that has deluded a great nation, and striven through its ruthless warcraft to fix a yoke of infamy on the whole world. Then will be the time to offer forgiveness if the fruits of repentance are brought forth, and such amends as are possible duly made. For a chastened and humbled, though not for a sullen and malicious Germany, there will be a place in a real brotherhood of the nations. She may sit with other states at the international council-board, and use for the common benefit her great gifts of deep thought, patient industry and skilful organisation. The world has need of her as long as she is content to be a member of a Family of Nations. She will discover that the Allies have no intention of depriving her of a rood of land that is really German, or crippling her by penalties more severe than what is needful for reparation and security. She will then perhaps begin to realise the greatness of the deception practised by her rulers when they assured her she was fighting for her own safety and freedom. While her future attitude remains doubtful she cannot expect much influence in shaping that organisation of the Society of Nations for peace which must be started as soon as the war is over; but if she frankly accepts the new order she may come in time to have a full share in the task of moulding and developing it.

Meanwhile the need of a new departure is pressing and the world cannot begin too soon to make preparations for it. The preliminary work of discussion is going on now in every civilised country, and the Conference which meets to make peace should derive great assistance from it. It will be, as we have seen, a Conference so big as to be fairly representative of civilised humanity, especially if the few powers of importance which remain neutral are given a consultative voice. If in addition the states which compose it resolve to shoulder the responsibility of enforcing International Law, we may look for some long steps forward in the direction of the organisation of the Society of Nations for peace, and against war. But the task of thinking out a practical form of such organisation is far too great and complicated to be performed by the body whose primary work it is to settle the conditions of peace. Still the initiative must come from the great representative Conference; for nothing short of the decision of the leading powers of the world will suffice to put so vast an enterprise in hand with any chance of success. The best solution of the difficulty appears to be that the Conference should lay down a few fundamental principles and ideas, and then appoint an International Committee to work out the details, and embody its proposals in a great Law-making Treaty which every power in the civilised world should be invited to sign. Another International Committee should be appointed to revise the Law of Nations in the light of the experience gained by the war, and produce an International Code. When the drafts are ready they should be submitted first to the government of each separate state, and finally to a great International Congress composed of representatives from all civilised states.

All this will take years to accomplish; but it is of the utmost importance that it should be begun at once, before the memory of the horrors of the World-War has grown dull, and while mankind are still suffering from the evils that arise from the neglect of the divine precepts of justice, mercy and brotherhood. It is not necessary, or even desirable, that the Committees we have suggested should be composed entirely of members of the Peace Conference. Many of them will possess no special qualifications for such service, and most will be too busy with their primary work of negotiating the conditions of settlement. The framing of a new world-order will tax the utmost energies of the best intellects and highest characters to be found among men. These should be selected for the purpose whether they are plenipotentiaries at the Peace Conference or not. They should be told the objects they are to aim at, and must then be left free to work out the best plans for attaining them in the existing condition of the world. On no account must they waste their time in constructing Utopias, and devising what seem to them flawless projects suited only for ideal conditions of human life. It should be understood that they will issue a series of Reports, each dealing with a different department of their subject, and a period of many months should be assigned to them for the purpose. One thing, however, must be done quickly, if it is to be done at all. Mankind cannot wait long for some means, however rudimentary, for settling international disputes without war. If they are delayed, fresh quarrels will soon break out; and the awful round of misery, bloodshed, torture and ruin will begin again, to the destruction of civilisation itself, which cannot endure a quick repetition of the horrors of the last few years. Either the Peace Conference must place foremost among the conditions of the great settlement a general obligation to submit disputes that cannot be settled by diplomatic means to some international authority or authorities, created by itself, or it must instruct the Committee it puts in charge of such matters to report on this question within three months at most, and must itself take immediate action on the recommendations it receives.

LECTURE VI.

THE REBUILDING OF INTERNATIONAL SOCIETY.

In the third and fourth of these Lectures we described the worst and most obtrusive of the evils existing in the Society of Nations. In the fifth we endeavoured to set forth the conditions precedent to the application of remedies with any prospect of success. We saw that civilised states must not be content with obeying International Law; but must in addition accept the duty of enforcing it on wrongdoers among their number, just as individuals in a state bring their combined force to bear on unworthy members of the community who break and defy its laws. This change from a passive to an active obedience must itself be effected by the common consent of civilised mankind, embodied in a great law-making international document, which must be signed and ratified in the most formal manner by those in each state who have authority to pledge its faith before the world.

It is clear that such an epoch-making act cannot be brought about without a great change of heart among the peoples. They must realise the brotherhood of nations in a way they have never done before. They must part for ever with the doctrine that right and justice, benevolence and good-will, have no place in the intercourse of states though they are essential to the well-being of the Society of Individuals. In short they must resolve to apply the principles of Christianity to their transactions with one another. The will to power must go and the will to serve must take its place. There can be no doubt that the war has brought about a great spiritual awakening in many circles; and even when no effects of this kind are perceptible mere prudence may do what the vision of a regenerated world has failed to accomplish. For the bitter experience of the last few years must surely have convinced the most sceptical that a continuance of present conditions will in no long time destroy civilisation itself. And the resulting barbarism will be much worse than that from which the race has slowly emerged, because it will have all the resources of science at the disposal of its spirit of violence and destruction. With this as the only alternative, men devoid of moral enthusiasm or spiritual vision may well resolve to give the precepts of Christ a trial in international affairs, simply on the ground that they may make things better, and cannot possibly make them worse. And though such people are useless as pioneers, as a wing of a great army slowly forcing its way onward against strong resistance they have a valuable function to perform. They prevent the rest from expecting the impossible. Enthusiasts for righteousness are the very salt of the earth, which would be rotten indeed if it were not for their health-giving activity. But they are apt to underrate difficulties, and ignore the fact that their own ardent nature is not widely diffused among men. It is well therefore to be sometimes reminded that we are not out in this present crusade to establish the Millennium by one great international treaty. No one who is of any serious account in the world of thought or action imagines that the coming Peace Conference can set up on earth the New Jerusalem,

> State serving State in joyful amity,
> Safe in the reign of Universal Law.

This is the ideal to keep before our eyes; but we know full well that the victories of justice and brotherhood are not secured in one supreme moment by one magnificent rush. Like victories in the field under the conditions of modern warfare, they must be fought for step by step. Sustained effort, long continued watchfulness, careful thought, and self-sacrificing endurance are necessary to win the gains within reach, much more therefore to hold and improve them, and prepare the final triumph.

And even when a new and better order has taken the place of the present defective organisation of international society, we must always remember that it will be but a piece of human machinery, and therefore by no means flawless. The law of even the most progressive states has its defects. Nevertheless life and property are far more secure, and justice is far better done between man and man, than was the case in the old days when each was his own avenger and righted his wrongs by the might of his own hands. No one now wants to go back to them. Whatever of evil may lurk in the law of the land and its administration, it is far more endurable than

> the good old rule,
> . . . . the simple plan,
> That they should take who have the power,
> And they should keep who can.[1]

So will it be with the Society of Nations. Its law will need alterations and additions from time to time, and precautions must be taken against bias and corruption among those who are charged with the task of interpreting and enforcing it. But the change from an international order based on the last resort on war, and at all times engrossed in costly preparations for war, to an international order based on justice and provided as a matter of course with Courts to administer it, will afford to rulers and peoples such a blessed relief from ruinous expense and constant anxiety that no self-governing state, even when smarting under the decision of a tribunal against it, will attempt to revive the discredited chaos of former days. Very possibly, nay, almost certainly, we shall not be able to establish all at once such a complete system as we should wish. But if only we can make a good beginning now, succeeding generations will take up the work in their turn, and develop further the beneficent institutions they will have inherited from us.

[1] Wordsworth, *Rob Roy's Grave.*

The means devised for securing the noble aims I have set before you is the foundation of a League of Nations in which all civilised states, or at least the greater number of them, shall be banded together for the purpose of settling international disputes without war. There is nothing new in a League. History positively bristles with examples. Again and again in all ages groups of states have entered into alliances, generally for some temporary purpose, such as the defeat of another state or states in war. We need go no further for a case in point than the present alliance against Germany and the Central Powers. Sometimes a more permanent object was contemplated, as when by the Achæan League in ancient Greece several city-states were banded together for the purpose of securing permanent peace among themselves, and common defence against external attack. Occasionally, though very seldom, the production of a new state from more or less independent elements has been aimed at. The most conspicuous instance is the creation of the United States of America out of the thirteen colonies who cut themselves adrift from Great Britain in 1776 and forced her to acknowledge their independence in 1783.

But the yet unformed League we have in mind to-day differs from all the formed and historical Leagues which have preceded it. They were partial. It is general in idea and we hope will be general in reality. It aims at nothing less than binding all the civilised states of the world together, and that permanently and not for a time only. But it does not seek to make of them one great world-state. Its promoters are not wasting strength and energy on the task of super-Empire building. They regard it as at once chimerical and reactionary; and undoubtedly they are right. Whatever a few enthusiasts may say, the idea of forming all peoples who have passed out of the stage of barbarism into one huge Confederation under one supreme government, with scores or even hundreds of subordinate authorities under it, is fantastic to the last degree. No attempt to realise it is likely to advance further than the paper on which the project is written. The ennobling passion of patriotism, which has been enormously strengthened by the events of the present war, would rise in revolt against it. Imagine, for instance, the feelings of the average Frenchman when told that *La Patrie,* for which he has suffered and bled, and for the freedom of whose sacred soil his nearest and dearest have gladly died, is to be reduced to the rank of a department in a new political entity, called, let us say, the United States of the World. The thing is impossible, as impossible as turning all Monarchies into Republics on the one hand, or on the other establishing an Universal Empire with William II of Prussia as its Emperor.

Moreover the notion is as reactionary as it is fanciful. Alexander may have dreamed of a world-state, and Napoleon of a great European Empire with Egypt and India and a large part of the East thrown in. But neither of these brilliant conquerors has been regarded as one of the heaven-sent leaders who have guided the bleeding footsteps of mankind along the stony way that leads to the promised land. Whatever may be the case centuries hence, neither to-day nor for long ages to come will the nations of the earth approximate to one another so closely in ideas and civilisation as to make possible one supreme authority over them all, even though it be limited in scope to a few functions. Any attempt to set up such an authority could proceed by force only, and would therefore intensify the evils it was meant to cure.

But while we cannot revive projects of world-wide sovereignty, and ought not if we could, the notion of duty to humanity at large needs to be strenuously insisted on. It ought to be developed side by side with the patriotic emotions. There is no real opposition between the two; but on the contrary those who are most devoted to their own land will generally be found more responsive than others to the claims of the race, just as within the state the best husbands and fathers are almost invariably the best citizens also. The glad and self-sacrificing performance of the duty of limited scope gives rise to joyful willingness to undertake the wider obligation. This point of view has been seized by M. Clemenceau, the veteran Prime Minister of France, and eloquently set forth in the noble words with which he greeted the victories of the French armies in the Summer of 1918: "The supreme obstacle to the establishment of right among mankind is about to disappear amid the pæans of a victory which it will be our duty to convert into a triumph for humanity. . . . Our nation, which has devoted so much of all its energies to all the causes of humanity, takes no account of its wounds. For long it existed without hope. It has earned its right to the day, so long awaited, that now has dawned, and it asks for no recompense but the privilege of working in common with all other nations of good conscience at the problems of social equity which will be the abundant fruit of the most splendid victory of all times."[1]

The most pressing of the services which the nations owe to the race at large is the reorganisation of international society, and the setting up in it of efficient machinery for the settlement of international quarrels. Unless we can in the immediate future make wars less frequent and less terrible and in the end abolish war altogether, all other reforms, all other attempts to realise social equity, will be useless. They will vanish amidst the storms of a bloody catastrophe in which civilisation itself will be shattered to pieces. M. Clemenceau has seen this; and though till lately he was not regarded as a strong supporter of the project of a League of Nations, recently, when declaring in favour of putting an end to violence and the introduction of the régime of organised law, he added the remarkable words, "The régime of organised law for the world is the League of Nations."[2] The French

[1] Message to the Presidents of the Departmental Councils-General, August 25, 1918.

[2] Account of Interview in *Daily Chronicle* of August 27, 1918.

Premier, therefore, interprets the task he so nobly and confidently accepts for his heroic people as including among the first of its reforms the establishment of a League of Nations. Nor does he stand alone. It is not too much to say that the leading statesmen in all the Allied governments share his view, and many of them hold it even more strongly than he does.

But it may be argued that such a League would derogate from the independence and sovereignty of the states which compose it. Undoubtedly it would take away from each member the right of deciding for itself on the spur of the moment whether it should resort to war when a dispute in which it was engaged failed to yield to diplomatic means of settlement. But would this limitation amount to a surrender of sovereignty? If so, then no state in the whole world is sovereign and independent; for there is none that has not bound itself in advance to take some particular course in certain circumstances, and has therefore parted to that extent with its absolute freeedom of action. Indeed we may go still further and say that quite apart from special agreement every state finds its activities constantly limited or stimulated by the mere fact of its membership in the Society of Nations. For states, and for individuals also, every advance in civilisation implies restraint. It is the price we pay for social life. Liberty in the sense of being free to do just what one pleases, how one pleases, and when one pleases, spells savagery. That man is free whose conduct is governed by rules which his own mind and conscience approve, because they are based on a due regard for the welfare of others as well as his own. Similarly that state is independent whose action is conditioned by no restraints save those to which it has freely submitted, in order to secure its own and the common good. Its sovereignty consists in freedom from habitual submission to the dictates of any external authority in matters of national policy and conduct, not in the power of riding roughshod over other states for its own selfish purposes. If this be correct, no state can lose its independence by entering a League, and covenanting with the other members to refer disputes between them to the decision of an impartial tribunal and to join in enforcing the rules of the League upon disobedient members. This is no new doctrine invented for the purpose of removing an objection against the project which is called for convenience' sake that of a League of Nations. It exists by implication in the current practice of states. No one of any account has ventured to impugn the full sovereignty and complete independence of Great Britain or the United States of America. And yet by the Clayton-Bulwer Treaty of 1850 these two powers bound themselves to each other not to make acquisitions of territory in Central America. The Treaty lasted till 1901, when under a new and entirely altered set of circumstances it was abrogated, and replaced by the quite different provisions of the Hay-Pauncefote Treaty. That is to say, for fifty years two of the strongest and most important states in the world submitted to a drastic restriction on the exercise of their right under International Law of adding to their dominions by conquest, occupation, or cession. Nor did such a transaction stand alone. The annals of diplomacy are crowded with similar self-denying ordinances. For instance, in the latter part of the last century the chief colonising powers of Europe made many agreements for the delimitation of their respective Spheres of Influence in the parts of Africa unoccupied by civilised peoples. In every case each party bargained for the reservation to itself of certain large districts, on condition that it did not in the districts reserved for the other "make acquisitions, conclude treaties, accept sovereign rights or Protectorates, or hinder the extension of the influence of the other."[1] To purchase a free hand in one quarter state after state submitted to severe restraints in another. And yet these states were never deemed to have parted with their independence. Neither has it been affected in the judgment of the world's rulers by adhesion to great international agreements whereby large groups of states pledge themselves to take in future certain action which ordinary International Law does not render incumbent upon them, or to submit in future to action on the part of others when ordinary International Law lays them under no obligation to do so.

The Geneva Conventions of 1864 and 1906 are good examples of the first kind, and the second is well illustrated by the General Act of the Brussels Confer-

[1] Anglo-German Agreement of 1890, Art. VII.

ence of 1890. By the former nearly all civilised powers have bound themselves to care for the sick and wounded of the enemy as well as their own, and to respect and protect all medical units and establishments to whichever side they may belong. By the latter a large number of states have agreed to the search, and if necessary the capture, of their merchantmen by the warships of the other signatory powers when they are suspected of being engaged in the Slave Trade, provided that the visit and search takes place in a certain well-defined maritime zone and is applied only to vessels of less than 500 tons. This involves a remarkable surrender; for by the Law of Nations every state has exclusive jurisdiction over its vessels on the high seas, and the right to search other ships than their own is jealously denied to all save belligerents, except in the case of pirates who may be visited and captured by the commissioned cruisers of any power. Yet in order to right a great wrong and rid mankind of a terrible scourge the leading maritime powers of the world have consented in this one case to allow officers of other nations to perform acts of high state authority under their flags. Had this been done as a mere act of power, it would have amounted to a gross infringement of their sovereign rights; but since they agreed to it beforehand they are no more deemed to have forfeited full independence thereby than a man who has applied for and received a post under a business firm is held to have forfeited his personal liberty by being obliged to keep office hours. And when the agreement is entered into for the welfare of the world the states who are parties to it, instead of being degraded thereby in the opinion of mankind, receive the reward of their self-sacrifice in fuller honour and a position of greater influence than before. The idea that entry into the contemplated League of Nations will derogate from the full independence of the powers who join it is due to a compound of bad jurisprudence and unhistorical history. In jurisprudence a general consent fully and freely given beforehand takes away the element of external compulsion and all that it implies; and in history power after power is recorded as having submitted to great restraints on its freedom of action without being regarded as having lost its position as a sovereign state.

But for all this we are by no means secure against an attempt to frighten patriotic citizens with the spectre of universal dominion. We must remember that the world contains a vast number of people who are by nature averse to change, and disposed to see nothing but the dangerous side of any projected improvement. If they could have had their way we should still be travelling by stage coach for fear of railway accidents, and writing all our business letters ourselves for fear of a breach of confidence on the part of a shorthand typist. Besides these there are others who feel instinctively that the new order must interfere with some pleasant practice of their own out of which they suck no small advantage, and are therefore blind to its evil effects on the community. Viscount Grey of Falloden, who it will be remembered was Foreign Secretary for Great Britain when the war broke out and for some time after, tells in his valuable pamphlet on our present subject an amusing story of an African chief in a territory under British rule. He strongly objected to paying taxes; and when it was pointed out to him that they were used to support a police force which kept order and prevented raids, he declared that he could protect his own tribe himself, and was able before the British came to raid his neighbours, and return in triumph with booty and captives, to the joy of all his people and the special delight of his womenfolk. "Now," said he, "you come here and tell me that I ought to like paying taxes to be prevented from doing this, and that makes me mad." [1] There are a few states and many individuals who resemble this black potentate in all things but his frankness. Prussia, for instance, has made of war a profitable industry, and openly and avowedly regards it as a political weapon, to be resorted to whenever its use is likely to be advantageous in that struggle with other powers which she regards as the right and indispensable condition of international society. As long as she is in this state of mind, which means in effect as long as her military power remains unshaken and on the whole victorious, she cannot be expected to welcome an attempt to establish a social order among the nations based on peace and good-will instead of conflict, and developed by impartial justice instead of the clash of arms. And on

[1] Grey, *The League of Nations*, pp. 11, 12.

her side among individuals will be those whose natures have been thoroughly Prussianised, that is to say, the arrogant, the masterful, the contemners of the Christ-like spirit, and also all those who find in war and preparations for war the means of gaining great positions and large fortunes, that is to say the army-contractors, the munition-makers, and the hunters after military glory for the fame and honour it brings. All these will raise the cry of National Sovereignty in Danger; and some of us, especially the timid folk who shrink constitutionally from any disturbance of the accustomed order, will really believe it. They will be joined by the fanatics of state equality, the publicists who would rather see right and justice assassinated in the international forum than secured by according legal recognition to the differences in power and influence which exist among the states of the civilised world. The united forces of these various contingents will put up a tremendous fight. In spite of such demonstrations as have just been given of the falsity of their battle-cry, they will muster large hosts at the polling stations and in the National Assemblies. Those of us who stand for national freedom and human brotherhood must meet them with the counter-cry of Civilisation in Danger. We need not shrink from the conflict. It will be a holy privilege to take part in it; and those who help to win the spiritual Armageddon will deserve as well of humanity as those who struck stout blows in the material Armageddon which is preceding it.

O that the armies indeed were arrayed! O joy of the onset!
Sound, thou trumpet of God! Come forth, great cause to array us!
King and leader appear! Thy soldiers sorrowing seek thee.[1]

But there need be no sorrowing in our ranks. Not only do we know under whose banner we fight: not only are we fully persuaded of the truth of what we believe: but we have found a leader. He is not an hereditary King, but an elected President, Woodrow Wilson, the chosen ruler of a hundred million American freemen. By his robust belief in freedom and humanity, his clear-eyed comprehension and eloquent presentment of the vital issues at stake, and his stern determination to use all the resources of his country for securing first complete victory and then righteous peace, he has roused the enthusiasm of the lovers of ordered liberty throughout the world; and by his wisdom, his strong sense of justice, and his unerring judgment, he has won the foremost place in the galaxy of able and devoted men who are directing the policy of the Allies. In his own stirring words he has convinced the champions of liberty and justice in this, the greatest struggle of all history, that "They are crusaders. They are fighting for no selfish advantage for their own nations. They would despise anyone who fought for the selfish advantage of any nation. They are giving their lives that

[1] Arthur Clough, *Bothie of Tober-na-Vuolich.*

homes everywhere may be kept sacred and safe, and men everywhere be free." [1]

That the man who can write such words as these should be acclaimed as prophet and leader by the foremost democracies of the world is a proof that the change of heart of which we spoke at the beginning of this Lecture has made great progress among men. Consciously or unconsciously they are being taught by suffering, and permeated by the spirit of Christ. To them is granted a glimpse of the goal of the world, which is, as a great divine has finely said, "to be the Kingdom of God established in the liberty of His children, through the service and sacrifice of love." [2] When once the peoples of the earth have seen this great vision of happiness through mutual service, and peace and security through brotherhood and justice, they will brush aside all quibbles about state sovereignty, and demand that the Society of Nations shall be so reorganised that in future disputes between its members must be settled without war. Their rulers will be told to create a League of Nations for this purpose, or give place to others who are willing to undertake the task. Then will be the time for the faint-hearted, the sceptical, and the partisans of enmity and force, to maintain that, splendid as is the idea of a free and peaceful world, the difficulties in the way of its realisation are insuperable. In what remains of this Lecture we will briefly consider such a plea.

[1] *Labour Day Message,* September 2, 1918.

[2] J. W. Oman in *Pain and Conflict in Human Life,* p. 170.

When proposals for reform have passed safely through the stage of being regarded as wicked or ridiculous, they are usually met with the objection that they are impracticable. But as a rule this accusation derives its power to dishearten and restrain from nothing more formidable than our own timidity. Readers of *Pilgrim's Progress* will remember how terribly Christian was frightened at first by the lions on either side of the pathway to the Celestial City. Yet when he plucked up heart of grace and went bravely on between them, " he heard them roar, but they did him no harm." Similarly when we see lions standing on guard along the road which leads to peace and freedom for mankind, the best and simplest course is to go straight on; and we shall probably find that the difficulties that look so formidable can be surmounted by care and courage, or even in some cases turn out to be no difficulties at all. At the present moment the lions are very busy, and there is much roaring. We are told in despairing or threatening tones that absolutely impartial tribunals cannot be found, that even if they were found strong and ambitious states would never accept adverse decisions in matters of great moment, and in short that sinister interests must in the long run prevail against any tendency on the part of nations to work together for the common good. In addition it is asserted that no effective means of enforcing the decrees of international tribunals can be established without general disarmament and the creation of an International Police Force under the orders of some central authority which does not exist and could not be called into being without first doing what is admitted to be impracticable and creating one great World-State. We shall, I think, find on examination that some of these so-called impossibilities have been recently performed, and others can be attempted with every prospect of success by developments and combinations of institutions already in existence.

If this be so, our League of Nations will prove to be but a further step in the gradual evolution of international society. It is of the utmost importance that every effort should be made to give it this character, not only in appearance but in reality. Nothing could be more fatal than to represent it as a wonderful device which will cure, by brand new remedies, a large part of the evils which afflict humanity, and has been perfected on the spur of the moment in the minds of modern champions of democracy as far superior in character and ability to the statesmen of past epochs as is the plan itself to the international chaos that preceded it. The peoples of the world shrewdly suspect that there is a great deal of political quackery about, and have no fancy for being made into its victims. But if they can be convinced that the step they are asked to take is a long stride forwards on a road which the best statesmen and the most progressive nations have been following for generations, they may be induced to brace their nerves and muscles for the bound. Nor will they be grievously disappointed if it does not land them at once at the goal of their efforts. Instead they will rejoice if it brings them perceptibly nearer, and in the meantime greatly improves their condition; and will be quite content to leave to their descendants both the toil of further progress and the happiness of a nearer approach to perfection. The earlier half of these Lectures will have been written in vain, if my readers are not convinced that a very real improvement in the international order took place during the last three centuries, and continued till its progress was suddenly arrested by the outbreak of the World-War in 1914. I will try now, at the end of the latter half, to shew how this improvement may be continued at a greatly accelerated pace by advancing on the old lines. We need not fear to innovate; but we must take care that the innovations are developments of plans and principles that have already stood the test of experience.

Surely there is nothing strange or revolutionary about a League. There have been such things since the beginning of recorded history. Latterly one has been growing up as big as civilisation itself; for what is the Society of Nations but a League of Nations, though it does not go by that name? We have seen that it has gradually become self-conscious through the machinery of Congresses and Conferences ever increasing in the numbers of the states represented and widening in the scope of the business transacted. At last in the Hague Conferences of 1899 and 1907 it evolved an organ for making something analogous to laws for the whole Society. In order to create an a demand on the part of Italy that the Sultan should cede to her a portion of the Turkish Empire, and involved the moral rather than legal question whether chronic and hopeless misgovernment on the part of one power can justify another in setting aside a legal title.

It follows from what has just been stated that for the settlement of justiciable disputes we require as near an approach to a Law Court as can be obtained in the present state of international relations; while for non-justiciable cases a small Committee composed of men of tried statesmanship, penetrating insight and wide sympathy, would give the best chance of satisfactory solutions. The contemplated League of Nations should therefore provide both. The performance of the first half of the task, which is concerned with the provision of Arbitral Tribunals, need not be very difficult. We have but to start where the Hague Conference of 1907 left off,[1] and complete the organisation of the Judicial Arbitration Court, which was abandoned unfinished then because of the impossibility of inducing some of the smaller states to accept anything less than absolute equality with the greatest in the composition of the Court. Various ingenious ways of overcoming this difficulty have been proposed since, among the most hopeful being the election of the judges by representatives of all the powers who become members of the League. Given the good-will which is a condition precedent of any advance, it ought not to be very diffi-

[1] See *ante*, pp. 75, 76.

cult to create the permanent High Court of Arbitral Justice which is wanted. But the use of it should not be made obligatory at first. What must be insisted on is that all the members of the League shall refer all the justiciable disputes they cannot settle between themselves to an Arbitral Court of some kind and abide by its decision. This is essential. Without it we shall not have made any real advance. But whether the tribunal be the so-called Permanent Arbitral Court established at the Hague Conference of 1899, or the new and really permanent Court that has yet to be created, or a Court established for the occasion by special agreement between the parties concerned, is a matter of comparative indifference. At first submission to judicial process may be rendered easier by the knowledge that the disputants have a choice of tribunals, and can even make their own. But doubtless after a time the powers will be convinced of the superior advantages of a Court "freely and easily accessible, composed of judges representing the various judicial systems of the world, and capable of insuring continuity in arbitral jurisprudence.[1] When this occurs all cases will naturally find their way to the tribunal best qualified to deal with them; and it will stand alone as the judicial organ of international society, or possibly it may become a great Arbitral Appeal Court, fully occupied with hearing important issues brought up to it from inferior tribunals, which will have been created to act as Courts of First Instance

[1] Draft Hague Convention of 1907 Relative to the Creation of a Judicial Arbitration Court, Art. 1.

and to settle smaller matters. We may be quite sure that if once a system of International Courts is made to work successfully it will develop rapidly.

We have now to consider how the non-justiciable cases can be met. They would prove in practice more difficult than the others because as a rule they stir the passions of nations far more deeply. But even with regard to them we need not despair of creating means of peaceful settlement on the lines of the development of existing institutions. They, or rather some of them, have been dealt with in recent years, though the procedure has not been so definite or the method so simple as in justiciable disputes. For a century or so there has existed a somewhat nebulous body, called the Concert of Europe, whose growth and functions were briefly described in the second Lecture.[1] We saw there that the Six Great Powers of Europe exercised for a long time a somewhat vague and ill-defined supervision over changes in the international order of Europe, especially though not exclusively in matters connected with the slow dissolution of the Turkish Empire. We saw further that during the last generation the group of Great Powers has been enlarged by the addition of two Non-European States—America and Japan. Thus the Concert of Europe grew into a World-Concert, but only for some purposes which may be roughly described as world-purposes. International difficulties which were purely European in character were dealt with as before. For instance, in 1912 the European Concert

[1] See *ante*, pp. 39-42.

took in hand the questions connected with the first Balkan War, and endeavoured to settle them in such a way as to avoid a general struggle. In this it succeeded, but only for a short time. A second Balkan War broke out in 1913, largely because Austria backed by Germany instigated Bulgaria to quarrel with its allies, and thus brought about the act of bad faith which inaugurated the fratricidal conflict. After a short and merciless struggle it resulted in the utter defeat of Bulgaria, and was ended quickly by the Treaty of Bucharest, which was practically dictated by the Central Powers in flagrant defiance of the principle of Nationality. Then violence and intrigue took the place of honest diplomacy. Events rushed on with terrific impact to a fearful catastrophe. All attempts on the part of Viscount Grey of Falloden to revive the Concert of Europe and use it as peace-maker were foiled by the deliberate purpose of Germany. The lesser Concert perished in the turmoil of a world-wide conflict in which its leading members took opposite sides; and with it fell the World-Concert also.

Undoubtedly this brief recital does not encourage us to think that we can find ready made to our hands in the Concert of Europe or in the World-Concert a satisfactory means of settling those deep-seated international quarrels which are not susceptible of judicial treatment. But it does show that in the course of ages the Society of Nations has thrown up an organ, however rudimentary in structure and imperfect in action, for dealing with such cases. Moreover this organ did sometimes give results which, if not ideally perfect, at least prevented terrible wars and modified existing arrangements in the direction of righteousness. This was the case when in 1867 Luxemburg was neutralised and Italy raised to the rank of a Great Power, and when in 1882 the pressure of the Powers induced Turkey to cede Thessalian territory to Greece. And in our own time we have seen the outbreak of war over the Morocco Question prevented in 1900 by the Algeciras Conference, which was the work of the Great Powers, and the first Balkan War brought to an end in 1913 by the Concert of Europe. These are no mean achievements, though they might have been greatly improved upon. Putting matters as low as possible they shew that a Committee acting informally as representing the whole body of civilised states can find tolerable solutions of difficult international problems, and that power in the hands of those who arrive at the solution is as essential to its success as the justice of the solution itself. What the world needs is a reform of the Committee which will make it really and formally representative of the whole Society of Nations, while at the same time there shall stand behind it, ready to be called into action if needed, the organised force of the entire community. If the states of civilised humanity were bound together in a great League such as we have contemplated, it should be possible to secure by election a competent Committee to deal with all cases that may arise, or a series of competent Committees each elected *ad hoc* for its own particular case.

But it seems to me that unless some position of advantage on the Committee or Committees is reserved for the Great World-Powers, we cannot be sure that predominant force would always be available to support, if necessary, the decisions arrived at. Yet unless this union of irresistible force with impartial justice can be established and maintained, the new order will break down, like the old, in a welter of bloodshed and misery. It subsists more or less completely in every decently governed state as far as the relations of individuals are concerned. Why should it be deemed impossible in the relations of states? Given the will to install right as the arbiter of international disputes the way seems fairly obvious.

But we must remember that nothing can be done unless states shoulder the obligation of enforcing International Law. If they are willing to add this to the duty already incumbent on them of obeying its rules themselves, it follows that our contemplated League of Nations must contain provisions for coercing recalcitrant members. There are economic and social means of bringing pressure to bear, and we may confidently hope that a resort to armed force will be rarely, if ever, required. But the force must be there, because without it, and the fixed intention of using it in the last resort, all other means will be valueless. A powerful and unscrupulous state could compel their abandonment by a vigorous use of its own forces. As soon as this was done the whole machinery of the League would be thrown out of gear and become useless, just as the social order within a state would collapse beneath the onslaught of armed brigands if the authorities had no police and no troops to use against them. Whether the force necessary to secure obedience to the decisions of the League's Tribunals should be a kind of sea and land police under the direct orders of the chief tribunal, or whether it should consist of contingents called up from each of the member states according to some plan agreed upon at the beginning, is one of those problems which should be left to the statesmen and jurists who will have to work out the details of the League's constitution. Civilised mankind will do well to trust much to such experts. The problems to be solved are far too complicated for the average citizen to deal with, ignorant as he must necessarily be of historical and technical details. He should be content to insist on a few great principles, and this he must do with no uncertain voice. If he shews that he is in earnest and will take no denial, trained and experienced masters of state-craft and law-craft will do his behests far better than he could do them himself. But he must be reconciled to the certainty that at first their work will be neither complete nor perfect. I trust they will not attempt to provide beforehand for every contingency that the mind of man can conceive. This is not the way the great contributions to human progress in the sphere of government are made. There would have been no British Parliament if Edward I and his advisers had endeavoured to think out and provide for all the problems of representation and control which have since arisen. Even the Constitution of the United States has received several amendments, and will no doubt receive in due time many more. It has also been modified in several respects by the almost imperceptible growth of political custom, as for instance with regard to the election of the President. What happens in the growth of institutions is that from time to time a great step forward is made consciously, and sometimes by a mighty effort and with much misgiving. Generally the impelling force has been the wish to escape from some calamity or secure some ardently desired benefit, often both combined. Then, when that immediate end has been attained with more or less completeness, the new institution has been slowly improved and developed by the wisdom of succeeding generations who have met their difficulties with new devices suited to the circumstances of their own times. So we may hope it will be with the League of Nations. It will be constituted to deliver humanity from the scourge of war, or at least to diminish its frequency and its terrors. If it succeeds in doing this to any considerable extent, it will be so precious to the nations that they will not permit it to succumb to any of the dangers that will undoubtedly beset its path. Instead they will provide means of providing against them as they arise, and thus gradually perfect the machinery of the League, sometimes in ways which do not now come within the scope of our vision. To gain the greatest results in the long run we must not ask too much at first. We must be content with deliverance from the evils that have well-nigh overwhelmed us in these last terrible years. But we must take care that the deliverance is thorough as far as it goes; and this it will not be unless it provides for the enforcement of the rules of the League by all the might of its members.

It is necessary also to secure that any force placed at the disposal of the final authority in the League shall be sufficient for the purposes in view. This means in practice that no member should be permitted to amass armaments at its own will and pleasure, and that a proportional reduction of present armaments should take place as soon as possible. Entire disarmament is not desirable, even if it were feasible. Each state will require a force to cope with internal disorders, and those whose frontiers march with territory inhabited by peoples too barbarous to be members of the League will need protection against their inroads. Similarly at sea trade will ask for security, and security cannot be obtained by merely proclaiming it. Pirates and slave-traders understand no argument but that of force. How to bring about proportional reduction of armaments is probably the most difficult of all the problems that await solution if the world is to be organised for peace, and not for war. One thing, and one thing only, seems quite clear in connection with it, and that is the absolute necessity of prohibiting all private trade in the manufacture and distribution of munitions of war. The state alone should be allowed to make and hold the means of deadly strife. Beyond this nothing can be said with certitude, save that some way must be found for " rationing " each state as to the nature and extent of its preparations for war. The discovery of the best means should be left to experts; and it should be recognised that their task must take a long time, and cannot be performed to perfection at the first attempt. We must be content in this, as in many other departments of life and conduct, with some tolerable approach to the end in view.

We have now seen that there are four needs, the satisfaction of which civilised mankind should insist upon in any scheme for the creation of a new and better international order whether by means of a League of Nations or in some other way. They are first the provision of Arbitral Courts to deal with cases susceptible of judicial treatment, secondly the establishment of Conciliation Committees for the settlement of cases not capable of legal adjustment, thirdly the organisation of an international force to be used in the last resort for the purpose of compelling recalcitrant states to submit to the decisions of these Tribunals and Committees, and fourthly the proportional and simultaneous disarmament of all civilised powers, saving only the forces necessary to safeguard the social fabric. The first of these can be satisfied by carrying a little further the plans already formulated and in part put into working order by the Hague Conferences of 1899 and 1907. The second could be met by the drastic reform and vigorous development of the system of the Concert of Europe and the World-Concert which has had a rudimentary and precarious existence for several generations. In dealing with the third we may obtain valuable hints from the few occasions when an international force was used to bring pressure to bear on a state which defied the Concert of Europe. As to the fourth there are no precedents; but proposals pointing to partial disarmament have been made by responsible rulers on several occasions, and as late as 1907 the Second Hague Conference passed unanimously a resolution to the effect that the serious examination by the powers of the question of the restriction of military charges was eminently desirable. All these are directly concerned with the organisation and work of the League.

But in addition it will be necessary to make provision for the revision of its activities from time to time, and also for the improvement and extension of the International Law under which it must live and which its Courts will have to administer. For this something in the nature of a Legislative Assembly will be required; and the nations already possess the germ of one in the Hague Conference. Many reforms are needed both in its constitution and in its procedure. But it has not to be created. There it stands, ready for adjustment to the needs of the new epoch.

Here then we have our answer to those who parade before us their pet bogie of impracticability. Some of the things that require to be done have been accomplished already. Others have come near to accomplishment. The experience of the past is full of guidance for the future. A little more courage, a little more confidence in humankind, a little more faith in God and goodness, and the field is won. The Faint-hearts always start some new scare when the terror of the first is removed. They now whisper with bated breath, "Look at the Holy Alliance. That was a League, and it became the instrument of a gang of despots for the purpose of riveting the yoke of autocracy on the peoples." From this they ask us to infer that a League of Nations must come to a like end, which is much the same as pointing to an unhappy marriage, and using it as an argument against the institution of matrimony. The League of Nations, if established, will become what its members want it to become. Its future must rest with them. Then we are solemnly warned of the danger of admitting Germany into the League, as if her permanent exclusion would not stultify the whole project, and give mankind, instead of one great organisation for maintaining peace, two hostile groups constantly plotting against each other and preparing for the inevitable struggle. It may well be that the conditions of admission for Germany should differ greatly according to her state of mind and mode of government at the time; but if she must be forced at all it would be far better to force her in than to bar her out. A repentant and regenerated Germany would be a valuable recruit for the brotherhood of nations; and a sullen and angry Germany would be much more efficiently restrained within the League than outside.

We come back at the end to what we have constantly asserted throughout. The problem before us is at bottom moral and spiritual. There is no real security for a better and nobler international society save the ennoblement of the thoughts and desires of men. The best constitutional machinery in the world will not produce good results if the citizens who work it are base and ignorant nor will the most ably-devised scheme for a League of Nations give to tortured humanity the peace and security it longs for if the nations themselves still cling to their old jealousies and schemes for mutual disservice. The more democratic the form of government in the separate states, the more completely will the nature of their international activities depend on the moral standard of their peoples. There is need therefore as political liberty extends of developing to the full that feeling of human brotherhood which is the great antidote to the poison of national hate. This feeling finds its home chiefly in the Church and in the Labour Movement. The union of the two in a demand for a League of Nations would make it irresistible, and at the same time purify it from all ignoble elements. Before the dim inarticulate peoples would arise a vision of world-righteousness and world-peace. Then in a flash they would realise that only the golden rule of Christ can bring the golden age of man. And what they see to-day they will obtain to-morrow; for

> The dreams which nations dream come true
> And shape the world anew.
>
> . . . .
>
> And down the happy future runs a flood
> Of prophesying light;
> It shews an earth no longer stained with blood,
> Blossom and fruit where now we see the bud
> Of brotherhood and right.[1]

[1] Lowell.

INDEX